DADLABS™

GUIDE TO FATHERHOOD

PREGNANCY AND YEAR ONE

CLAY NICHOLS, BRAD POWELL, TROY LANIER,
and OWEN EGERTON

QUIRK BOOKS

PHILADELPHIA

Library of Congress Cataloging in Publication Number:
2008938991

ISBN: 978-1-59474-318-4

Printed in China

Typeset in Blender and Clarendon

Designed by Headcase Design
Cover photograph by Caroline Mowry
Illustrations by Joel Holland
Contributing photography by Troy Lanier, Clay Nichols,
and Aaron Segura
Edited by Mindy Brown
Production management by John J. McGurk

Distributed in North America by Chronicle Books
680 Second Street
San Francisco, CA 94107

10 9 8 7 6 5 4 3 2 1

Quirk Books
215 Church Street
Philadelphia, PA 19106
www.quirkbooks.com

CONTENTS

PROLOGUE:

THE SOFA AT THE CENTER OF THE UNIVERSE

Sex: Is it worth it?

Legitimate question, and one many ask on the eve of a positive pregnancy test. She's pregnant, and you, like it or not, are now a full-fledged participant in a sexual revolution. It's a sexual revolution that sneaks up on you when you are lying on the sofa minding your own business. It's a sexual revolution that asks you to develop skills in nurturing, caretaking, and big box baby store shopping. It's a sexual revolution that offers men the chance to be involved in the lives of their children like never before.

With all these crazy changes going on, you're probably thinking: Maybe our forefathers were right. Maybe a man's place during delivery should be in a smoky "stork club," reading the newspaper instead of holding the laboring mom's knee and watching the baby "crown" (our nominee for best euphemism of all time). The dads of today look to the fathers of yore for wisdom on changing diapers and 2 A.M. feedings, and the old guys shake their grizzled heads and laugh at us.

The dads of the Old School may chuckle at the fact that we have been to the OB/GYN so many times that we have favorite chairs, that we can read ultrasounds, calm a colicky baby with deep squats at dawn, and quickly categorize poop as seedy or mustardy. But would modern dads trade? Would we set the clock back to a time when men were less involved with every detail of raising children? To that we say: Fuck rhetorical questions.

Suffice it to say, fatherhood has changed. What was rare a decade ago, and unheard of in generations past, is today's Standard Fatherhood Procedure. We've evolved, depending on your perspective, from breadwinner to part-time assistant parent to co-parent. Astonishingly, dads have discovered that washing bottles won't make your balls fall off, nor does folding laundry or taking the kid to the doctor. We've found out that being a good dad and a good fan are not mutually exclusive; that we aren't required to listen to Neil Sedaka, or give up beer entirely (hi, honey).

SAY HELLO TO DAD 2.0

There is no use denying that the balance of domestic responsibilities in the typical family household has shifted. So quit pretending you're asleep! It's your turn. While Dad 2.0 may laugh at the discomfort he feels at trying something gender awkward (e.g., braiding your daughter's hair before school), we roll in our dad way. We're getting it done, and getting better at it all the time.

In the abstract, the rewards of being Dad 2.0 can be a little tough for guys to buy into. The payoff for greater involvement with your children, after all, is an emotional one. All that work and loss of sleep, all in exchange for some kind of . . . feelings? It would be like your boss paying your bonus in dog biscuits—an enticing reward perhaps, just not for a guy. But as any Dad 2.0 will tell you, the rewards, when they come, are real and rich indeed. "Epic emotional attachment is not something we're ready for as guys," observes Kurt Voelker, a writer/director and dad living in Los Angeles. "But when my child sees me and jumps in my arms? Pure gold."

You may even begin to feel a little sad for those well-rested, TV-sports-enabled, butt-paste-free 1.0 Dads. A little jealous maybe, but on the whole glad to be one of the new models.

With all this nurturing and diaper changing and being present, is there some kind of big sociological trend worthy of the cover of *New York Times Magazine*? Are Dads the New Moms?

In a word: no. And we pretty much hate anyone who asks that question. Dads are not moms, and that is why there is this book. Men are not women, although they are involved in parenting from the moment of conception like never before. So we have questions about pregnancy, labor and delivery, and bringing home the baby, but these aren't the same questions that women have.

In the end, we think the biggest change in becoming a dad is that you get kicked off the metaphorical sofa at the center of the universe. It's not just about you anymore. Your needs are no longer your number-one priority.

They may not even make the top five—which can be a tough adjustment for us guys. Self-sacrifice, giving up the familiar and comfortable patterns of life—this is the price you pay for the rewards you get, as you'll soon find out.

Would we trade? Would we turn back the clock on fatherhood? Should writers answer rhetorical questions that call for time travel and could get them in trouble with their wives? We think not.

These changes take some work, some rehearsal, so for the next few months get up from that couch and give your spot to your pregnant wife.

OUR PANEL OF EXPERTS

Way back when we first got sucked into this whole parenting thing—er, got the good news that our wives were expecting—we were shocked about how little was out there for guys. Most of what we found that had any useful information was dry as Salt Lake on a Sunday or had just been repurposed from pink to blue, so to speak. What follows is our attempt to remedy that situation.

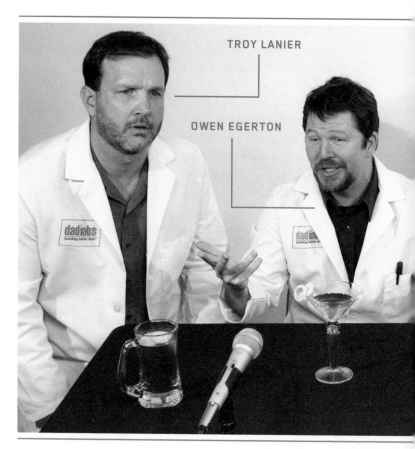

TROY LANIER

OWEN EGERTON

You may notice that we lack lots of letters after our names. No doctors here. No "experts." Just veterans. Our research department: We've got nine kids ranging in age from newborn to ten years. If there are any mistakes that we suggest avoiding, it's only because we've already made them. Collectively we've expected nine times, and talked with countless other dads about their experiences in this process. So what follows are all the things that we wish a guy had told us.

We screwed up, so you don't have to. Just ask our wives.

BRAD POWELL

CLAY NICHOLS

9

CHAPTER 1

SHUT UP, YOU'RE EXPECTING

NEWLY PREGNANT AND LYING YOUR ASS OFF

"There is no try. Only do. Or do not."

–Yoda

One of the first values that your parents probably tried to instill in you as a child was respect for the truth. Remember that thing with the Oreos? And how ashamed you felt, and how you finally decided to always tell your parents the truth? Super, but now that you're about to become a parent yourself, it's time to forget all that.

Conception and early pregnancy are awkward phases for prospective parents, and as a result, fibs, little white lies, and/or bald-faced whoppers will almost certainly be called for. After the child comes along, you can get your George Washington routine working just in time to have your own Oreo conversation. In the short term, you may want to model yourself on more contemporary politicians. Keep in mind:

12

- For married couples, a pregnancy of the unexpected variety may call for less lying overall.
- For unmarried couples, the opposite is probably true.
- For most would-be breeders, getting pregnant requires a pleasurable but socially delicate phase of "trying."

Some couples love to talk about how hard they are trying. They may even talk about ovulation cycles and temperatures and the viscosity of vaginal fluids (all ways to predict the "ideal moment" for conception). Is this really the best dinner table conversation? Instead, you should start lying. Not only will everyone at the dinner party be grateful, but you also spare yourself the potential embarrassment down the road when you are still trying several months later. On average it takes healthy couples in their twenties five cycles of ovulation to conceive, and, as a general rule, the older you are, the longer it takes. It's best to anticipate trying over a period of several months.

Avoid the "ick" factor of talking about your conception life in public while also ducking potentially awkward situations with infertile couples or couples with fertility issues. When you start trying, start lying.

SEX IS INVOLVED

"Trying" is awesome, by the way: a second honeymoon, spiced up with a sense of purpose. The frequency during this period of almost obligatory sex is something to look back on fondly during those first few months after Mom and baby come home from the hospital.

But that's getting ahead of ourselves.

13

- *Plan on having sex.*

For some guys, there is a downside to trying. If several cycles go by without pregnancy, be prepared for the mom-to-be to get a bit prescriptive about the wheres and whens of sex. She may be taking her temperature to determine the timing of her ovulation and may expect you to perform when the time is right. This might feel somewhat forced, mechanistic, anti-romantic, or even mercenary.

- *Focus on the sex.*

If you are truly exhausted or unready or just not that into it when your ovulating partner decides it's go time, and you decide to exercise your completely legitimate right to decline a sexual encounter, be ready for some push back. Your refusal will be perceived as a particularly stinging bicameral rejection: an insult not only to her attractiveness, but also to her ambitions to be a mom. By saying "no" to this particular sex, you will be harshing on all of her archetypes from mom to sexpot, and this could have lasting consequences.

- *Have the sex.*

Not to scare you or anything, but you really should be storing up.

SWIM LESSONS:
MALE FERTILITY FACT AND FICTION

There are two ways you can go with information about male fertility. Nice guys will use the following information to maximize fertility and thereby hasten things along to the stated goal of knocking the girl up. Other guys might use this information to prolong the not unpleasant process of "trying." We remain neutral on this issue.

* *In general, leading a healthier lifestyle will result in increased fertility.*

Your sperm like it when you eat foods rich in anti-oxidants or take supplements that contain anti-oxidants (a multi-vitamin will probably do the trick). They also appreciate it when you stay well hydrated. The system also works best when it is kept in regular use, but not overtaxed. Your sperm counts will be highest when you have one ejaculation every 24 to 48 hours. Less often than that and the number of dead and dying sperm in each ejaculation increases; more often than that and the sperm count is depleted. There may be some leverage here. You could call it fertility therapy, or motility maximization, or [insert your preferred euphemism here].

* *On the spermicidal side, heavy use of alcohol, tobacco, and especially marijuana will significantly depress your counts.*

Which presents an obvious conundrum. What's more important: mood or motility?

* *Vibration over an extended period will also negatively impact male fertility.*

So who signed up for that study? This means that long-haul trucking and daylong cruises on the chopper will not move you along the road to fatherhood. Excessive exercise has also been shown to contribute to lower sperm counts, so marathoning and baby-making may be incompatible.

* *The biggest enemy of male fertility is heat.*

Hot tubs are the biggest culprit, but you might want to avoid saunas; long, hot bubble baths; and even really hot showers. Anytime you are submerging your junk in hot water, you are bumping off swimmers by the millions.

Does all this mean that taking bong hits in the hot tub is a good form of birth control? No.

But isn't it pretty to think so?

● *How about the classic boxer vs. briefs debate?*
Does wearing tighty-whities ding the sperm count? Studies show that the style of undergarment does not significantly impact fertility, yet questions remain: What medical researchers decided to take their career down this path? Who volunteered to be studied? How can we ever thank these brave pioneers?

There are also those who believe that some sexual positions—missionary, for example–are better for procreation because sperm are deposited closer to the cervix. No medical proof for this theory exists, which is good because it raises uncomfortable questions about just how close to the cervix a guy can get.

CAN YOU INFLUENCE YOUR BABY'S SEX?

To one degree or another, most expecting dads we've talked to express a boy or girl preference. Some say things like, "I couldn't handle a girl" or "I don't need a little me running around." We may have even said a few things like that ourselves. But in our experience, kids tend to defy our expectations and stereotypes, to blow up our apprehensions, and to generally make themselves loved regardless. You will be surprised by your ability to care for a child whose gender makes you more nervous.

Still really want a boy or a girl despite our sage reassurances? Okay, then.

1. You can throw money and tech at the problem. Using methods developed by fertility specialists, you can deploy invasive techniques that can determine a baby's sex. Most of these procedures will not be covered by insurance, and expenses could run into the tens of thousands. If you are willing to plonk down that kind of cake just to have a daddy's little girl, you are most likely a wack job.

2. There are also a couple of contradictory and highly disputed "at home" methods. These "techniques" for influencing the gender outcome are premised on the observation that "male" sperm are faster swimmers but "female sperm" live longer. By carefully calculating the moment of ovulation by monitoring Mom's temperature and having sex at the appropriate moment, these methods suggest you can time the arrival of the desired type of sperm.

3. Then there are the wives' tales, which, while completely unsubstantiated, might be worth a try, just to keep things interesting (see page 18).

The medical community is in general agreement that these methods do have a success rate of at least 50 percent.

Just remember, if you don't get the outcome you want, you have no one to blame but yourself. It's the sperm that determines a baby's sex. And there is only one lead-pipe lock for getting the outcome you want: adoption.

OLD WIVES' TOP HOT SEX TIPS

- Do it standing up or "doggie style" for a boy
- Do it missionary style, or woman on top, for a girl
- Have sex at night for a boy, during the day for a girl
- Do it on odd calendar dates for boys, even days for girls
- Have sex with you climaxing first for a boy; with your partner climaxing first for a girl. (If this were true, what would the population look like?)

To summarize:
- Standing up, on the night of the fifth, you first, for a boy
- Her on top, on the morning of the sixth, her first, for a girl

18

KEEPING IT POSITIVE:
PREGNANCY TESTING FOR MEN

So, your wife or partner missed her period; it's time to cue the home pregnancy test. Some say that the road to fatherhood begins in the boudoir. Sure. But pregnancy really starts in the can.

Back in the day, there was hope and guesswork to determine whether a woman was pregnant. Today, not so much. Late first-trimester blood tests for pregnancy are pretty much things of the past. Today, highly accurate and simple-to-use home pregnancy tests are about as hard to come by as Pepto Bismol, and most work using a similar formula (though you should still read the instructions).

1. In most cases, the would-be mom will place the business end of the stick into her urine stream (morning pee is the best because it is the most concentrated).

2.   The urine is then exposed to an antibody attached to a pigment molecule that reacts with the pregnancy hormone hCG.

3.   This hormone, released as soon as the placenta begins to grow, is usually measurable six to ten days after conception. If hCG is present in the urine, then the stick will give you a sign: blue lines, a plus sign, a smiley face (not kidding). Reading the instructions is key to avoiding misunderstandings.

Regardless of a positive or negative outcome, you may be tempted to retest once, twice, several times. Once you have a positive test, however, retesting is just putting your money where your pee is. Manufacturers claim 99 percent accuracy, and charge accordingly. Some tests are pretty expensive—a high-end three-pack will set you back quite a lot of pocket change. There is no need to retest multiple times, but you probably won't listen to this advice because of all the adrenaline. No hard feelings.

In the case of a negative test, on the other hand, a recheck in a few days is not a bad idea. In some pregnancies, it may take a while for the hCG to build up to detectable levels.

PREGNANCY TEST SIDE EFFECTS

Close exposure to a freshly positive pregnancy test has been shown to cause a range of side effects in adult males, including:

- Gasping
- Dizziness
- Shortness of breath
- Spastic dancing-like movements of the arms and legs
- Elation
- Laughing
- Extreme depression

19

- Sense of impending financial doom and loss of time to watch sports
- Also, loose stool

Some may experience all of the above in rapid succession.

Although any and all of these side effects are perfectly normal, it's good to bear in mind that the now officially pregnant mom may be having a few side effects of her own.

So here again, lying comes into play.

If you are feeling anxieties about your fitness to be a father, the financial impact of having kids, your paternity, or poker night, the moment of "finding out" may not be the opportune time to explore those feelings. It is extremely important in the course of a parenting partnership for everyone to express their feelings and concerns openly. Just not right now. Give it 48.

It is truly a moment when the feelings come at you in packs. The excitement and the awesome responsibility of it all mix to rocket you up and weigh you down at the same moment. You are ecstatically encumbered. The brilliant, terrifying words "I'm gonna be a dad" will echo in your ears for a good long while.

One side effect that is extremely common and requires immediate treatment: an impulse to call Mom.

You're a good boy. You love your mom. You call her every Sunday. You've dealt patiently with her subtle-as-a-charging-mastodon hints about wanting grandkids for years. Now, finally, positive pregnancy test in hand, you can get her off your back. With one simple phone call. She will be delighted, and all good sons like to delight their mothers.

But your wife will be pissed. To be more precise, your newly pregnant wife will be pissed. And this is not a good outcome.

WHY NOT TELL?

• *Why would she be mad?*

The positive test is right there for everyone to see. WTF? Why not just tell the parents and grandparents at least? There are reasons, both emotional and medical.

The medical reason that many couples delay telling friends and family about a new pregnancy is the risk of miscarriage. Only a small percentage of pregnancies end in miscarriage (an important natural process that is often the result of genetic problems with the fetus). However, most miscarriages occur in the first trimester. After the fourth month, the risk falls off significantly.

It is this fact that gives shape to the traditional period of radio silence. Twelve weeks. The first third (trimester) of the 36 weeks (give or take) of pregnancy. Not telling spares a couple the process of later explaining that a pregnancy has ended in miscarriage.

• *Yes, but it's just my mom we're talking about!*

Not anymore. That relationship just got more complicated. The newly pregnant mom feels remarkably vulnerable, nervous—excited, too, but nervous. Unless she has an exceptionally close relationship with your mother, she may well feel insecure. Your mom has been through this (obviously) and may have opinions about the "right" way to do things. Rightly or wrongly, the expecting mom may not want input from your mother and may want to feel some degree of control over her own pregnancy, particularly at the outset.

• *Is being secretive normal?*

Yes. Your partner might want to set her own terms. Whom and when she tells about her pregnancy may have outsize importance. She may also want to share the moment exclusively with you, for at least a while. Keeping this secret can be good times.

A FIELD GUIDE TO LYING

If, as a couple, you do decide to delay telling people, it's time for you to get serious about lying. Getting fully behind this decision sends an early signal about your commitment to your wife/partner, the baby, and your fatherhood. You need to get up for some serious bullshitting.

Which brings us to another very good reason not to go broadcasting that you are trying to get pregnant: If you tell people you are trying, then you have to expect to be peppered with questions

DAD RANT

DADDY CLAY

When it was finally time to break the news, my wife and I decided to make a production of it. Our oldest child was the first of his generation on either side of the family, so we knew it would be a pretty big deal, plus both sets of parents were relentlessly lobbying for grandkids (we waited until our late twenties to have children).

It was around Christmas, and we had plans to travel to see both sets, so the time was right in terms of fairness (this was becoming increasingly important). Both sets of expecting grandparents would receive notification within hours of each other, in an essentially similar ceremony.

Before dinner (no wine with the meal would have been a dead giveaway for us), we sat the folks down and broke the news.

Although I believe both sets of parents were equally excited to hear the news, their respective responses were distinctly regional (I'm from Texas, my wife's from Massachusetts). In my memory, my parents let out an ear-piercing whoop and did a kind of wild do-si-do with high kicks and spinning that pretty much scared the crap out of my wife. My wife's parents shared a warm smile, then my father-in-law clapped a hand on my shoulder and said, "Now, that will change your tax picture."

Both sets of grandparents are similar in disputing my account vociferously every time I tell the story.

about whether or not you are pregnant yet. Friends start watching you, and particularly your partner, like a hawk.

- Does she have a drink?
- Is she not drinking?
- Why is she not drinking?

(We strongly recommend a prop drink—even a glass of wine from which to take fake sips.)

You know that your buddies will be just dying to find out. Especially the ones who already have kids. They can't wait to tell you nightmare stories, harass you, the usual. Fooling them will be hard because they know you. Unlike your wife's friends who will ask leading questions, your boys will put the question to you directly and scrutinize your face for any hint of a reaction. You can try to avoid the question, if you think you are a good enough politician. Try to say the following phrases with a straight face:

- "Pregnant? Now *that* would be exciting."
- "Pregnant? Can you imagine *me* being a dad?"
- "Pregnant? You know something I don't?"

But your buds will see right through them like a backlit sundress. One hint of a smirk, one wink, and the word is out—you're dead meat. Your wife is looking at you, hurt and betrayed: "You told them?" And you stammer and feel like crap.

Don't get cute. Don't try to be subtle. Don't walk a fine testimonial line. Lie. Lie your ass off. Look your friends straight in the eye and say, "We are not pregnant." Flat out, declarative sentence.

Will someone get their feelings hurt because you weren't telling them the truth—that you were actually pregnant when you said you weren't? No. Everybody knows you get a pass on this one.

CHAPTER 2

STIRRUPS AND SYMPATHY

A GUY'S GUIDE TO GYNECOLOGY

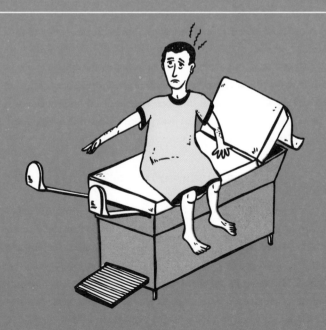

Probably, you are enlightened and mature. You're secure in your sexuality. The mechanics of childbirth are a beautiful and natural process worthy of respect and celebration. You can say "vagina," no problem. Good for you. You can probably skip this chapter.

EXPECTING YOU

On the other hand, somewhere in you may be lurking a fifteen-year-old boy. Find that boy. Introduce yourself to him. Reacquaint yourself for a moment, then bring up the subject of a gynecologist's office. An obstetrician/gynecologist, more specifically. Toss in a reference to stirrups, and step back for a minute.

What's that boy doing?

If the kid is cringing, changing the subject, or blowing milk out his nose, you may be feeling a bit uncomfortable about your wife's first visit to the OB/GYN. That's because *you* are going, too.

That's right, my friend. You are going to the OB/GYN office. And not just once, either. In the course of a normal pregnancy, an expecting mom may visit the doctor as many as a dozen times. It should be your goal to be at every single one of those appointments (especially for a first-time dad).

REMEMBER THOSE "OPTIONAL" PRACTICES?

Historically, men have not been encouraged to go to gynecologists' offices. Ask your dad how many visits he has made to the OB/GYN's office. When he finally stops laughing, it may be useful to remind yourself that this is a sign of progress. It is a privilege to accompany your wife on these appointments; to be present and participatory, a witness to a miracle. That turning back the clock is not something to be desired, or even possible.

26

Being bitter at this point is going to be counter-productive.

Men did not really become regulars at OB/GYN appointments until the 1990s. Doctors estimate that fathers are now present for about 30 percent of all appointments, up from only 5 percent a generation ago. The trend points to a tectonic shift that has taken place in the space of just a few years—men becoming full partners in the business of raising kids.

There are many possible explanations for guys showing up at the Home of the Pap Smear:

1. That this is some kind of echo boom from the change in roles that women have been undergoing for generations. If women can be expected to be in the boardroom, then guys should be in the exam room.

2. That the fragmentation of the American family—with expecting moms miles from their own mothers—has forced dads to sub for missing female relatives.

3. That maybe we've just wised up. Maybe guys just figured out that being shown the door when it comes to pregnancy, labor and delivery, and raising kids was a bad deal. That men should have equal access to the experiences and relationships everyone knows are the most important in life. How much do you really like your boss? Is more time with him or her really that important? More guys than ever define success as "spending more time with the family." If that is the case, then the ground floor of success is a gynecologist's office.

WHERE DID ALL THE BROWNIE POINTS GO?

The truth is that in the last few years, attending OB/GYN appointments (along with about a million other parenting responsibilities) has become a societal assumption. Sorry, Dad, we kind of volunteered you for this shit—which means you don't really get much credit for going. What was cause for comment and praise just a few years ago has become a simple expectation. You're probably not even going to get a nice, approving smile from the cute receptionist.

But that doesn't mean there isn't a wealth of really good reasons why you should be present:

1. The PR angle.

These appointments are an opportunity to make an early bid for full partnership status. Attendance at even the most mundane appointment lets Mom know that you support her and that you want to contribute to the process to the extent that you can. You should also remember that she's nervous, too. Not about the OB/GYN office, like you, but about all the information and unknowns that lie ahead. You will be a reassuring presence. Holding her hand is important.

2. The live-feed angle.

The doctor is a very efficient source of information. Rather than getting lots of info secondhand from Mom or from books/videos/Web (present authorship excluded), go to the source. Your doctor has practice presenting the information you need in a way that is digestible. Attending doctors' appointments is actually the most time-efficient way of staying informed.

3. The entertainment value angle.

Some doctor visits are amazing. Many of the most jaw-dropping, touching, heart-pounding moments of pregnancy happen in the doctor's office. Think about hearing the baby's heartbeat for the very first time or seeing an ultrasound reveal the image of a baby's hand. Is there really anything at the office that can match that?

GYNECOLOGICAL ENVIRONS

You've done it. You're in. OB/GYN—the whole deal. You hold the door of the office open for the pregnant mom and step in. You have a moment of being proud of yourself, then you begin to wonder what exactly you got yourself into. You wonder: Is there any place less appropriate for me to be? Women's Lingerie section at Sears? Why not spend your spare time at the hairdresser? What business has a guy got in a gynecologist's office?

A glance around reveals that the place is pretty much generic Doctor's Office, though like women's restrooms they tend to be a lot nicer than the male equivalent. The waiting room may have a few more plants and pastel colors than the proctologist's, but the basic layout is likely to be the same.

Stand with your wife in the line to sign in, and take in the scene. There will be moms with new babies, women in for check-ups, women in various stages of pregnancy, and probably even a smattering of other dudes. Take some comfort in observing their discomfort.

As your wife signs in, you may begin to suspect that the staff is genuinely glad that you are there. No alarms triggered by testosterone-sensing devices linked to Chick Central have sounded. The seats are quite comfy. No *SI*, but take this as an opportunity to check out *Modern Pregnancy* without fear of wiseass comments. You might even want to take a copy with you into the exam room when Mom is called back. It can provide handy cover.

The mom's name is called, and you get a little jolt. Time to go behind the curtain.

INTERNAL EXAM FOR EXTRA CREDIT

Given the situation, you have clearly accomplished a level of intimacy with your partner. Well done. But you are about to embark on a journey of discovery that will take your relationship to new depths.

Allow us to rephrase.

The miracle of pregnancy, labor, and delivery will almost certainly instill in the expecting dad an appreciation of the miraculous potential of a woman's body. An appreciation of miraculous potential is not, however, all that sexy. As a modern due dad, you are likely to be issued an invitation to a wide variety of gynecological procedures employing a number of tools, both technological and mechanical. Some dads will readily accept every invitation, while others will attempt gracefully to decline in an effort to "preserve the magic" (good luck).

What follows are some highlights from the OB/GYN playbook, so you can decide if you want a seat on the 50-yard line or a partially obscured view in the upper deck.

1. Backless gown and tumbler.

Each appointment begins with the same ritual:

- While Dad waits in the exam room, Mom visits the small but clinically well-appointed bathroom to slip into something less comfortable, and to make a deposit.
- She emerges in a surgical gown and bearing a urine sample in a cup.
- Some dads are tempted to comment: "Everything come out all right?" etc., etc. Others find conversation with a woman holding a cup of pee to be awkward.

Why the ritual? These aren't mere formalities. The gown makes examining the expecting mom easier for the doc, and the pee in the cup will be tested for indications of complications like gestational diabetes.

2. Vitals information.

The nurse handles some preliminaries including taking vitals, asking a few questions, and noting Mom's weight. The latter is a fraught moment—some moms will elect to turn away from the scale while the measurement is taken. This is really the perfect moment for dads to Shut the Hell Up. Things can only go bad for you. Almost no comment, regardless how well intentioned or supportive, will have the desired effect.

Why the weigh-in? If moms gain too much weight, they are at increased risk of birth complications, and bigger moms make bigger babies. We often equate big with healthy when it comes to newborns, but overweight babies are as likely as underweight babies to have postnatal issues.

3. Assuming your positions.

With the arrival of the doctor or midwife comes the main event—the "internal" or pelvic exam.

- Mom sits on the exam table.
- The doc whangs the bare metal stirrups from their hiding spot in the table, snaps on gloves, and drops on a little lube–keeping the patter going the whole time.
- About the time Mom gets her feet in the stirrups, you have made a decision about where in the room (or not) you want to be. If you are feeling uncertain, bring a magazine just in case you need the distraction.

4. Responses across the speculum.

The exam is usually very quick:

- One hand palpates the lower abdomen while the other goes under the gown. The doc inserts two fingers into the vagina, checking the condition of the cervix.
- If the doctor requires a look at the cervix, he or she may opt to use a speculum. This tool looks like two chrome spatulas attached to a caulking gun. The doc lubes and inserts this tool and clicks the trigger a few times, retracting the walls of the vagina to allow an unobstructed view of the cervix.
- Then it's over. The gloves are popped off and the Q&A continues.

DAD RANT

DADDY ~~~~~ CLAY

"If you'll step over here, you can see where the cervix is irritated." This is not a statement I had even imagined I would ever hear. My wife is on a table with her feet in the air, and a doctor is waving me over to have a look at her cervix. I froze and stammered. What's the protocol here? Should you ask your wife's permission? "Honey, can I look at your cervix?" Should I play it cool like I look at her cervix all the time? Go all clinical and doctor-like?

My grip on the copy of *Fit Pregnancy* I had been hiding behind tightened. My policy was always to remain in the exam room during these appointments, but to stay engrossed in periodicals during the actual exam.

Is declining really an option? "No thanks, dude, I'm all good for cervix right now." Is it more embarrassing to my wife for me to look, or to act like it would be gross for me to look? It's a no-win, and I'm getting a little pissed at the OB/GYN for putting me in this position.

And by hesitating, I've clearly blown it. Eventually I decide that I'll try to recover and look casual and mature, that the doctor is a woman makes a difference somehow, and that she's trying to explain something that is of concern. So I ask my wife later if that was the right thing to do. She said that it didn't much matter—my look of panic made it all worth it.

Why the cervical exam? The cervix ensures that everything and everyone stays where it/he is supposed to until the big birth day. The medical types monitor the cervix because any changes in thickness or aperture may be cause for concern.

At the end of each appointment the doctor, nurse, or midwife who has conducted the exam will ask if you have any questions (if he or she doesn't, you might want to look into changing your care). Have a canned question or two ready to go. Ask about nutrition, ask about fetal development, ask about the safety of household cleaners. Don't ask if you can have sex. You should know the answer to that.

LABOR INTENSIVE:
DITCHING WORK FOR OBSTETRICS

Okay, going to all the OB/GYN appointments is a beautiful ideal, but this is the real world and somebody has got to pay the Babies-R-Us bill. If work is an unavoidable reality, and you have to prioritize, go 1-3-2.

1. The doctors appointments in the first trimester are a must, with highlights like Doppler (not just for weather anymore) and ultrasound. (More on those in a minute.)

3. In the third trimester you are developing your game plan for the birth.

2. The appointments in the second trimester are primarily about tracking progress.

So in terms of prioritizing, it's a good idea to go ahead and cash in your chips in the first trimester, see if you can build up a stack in the second, and go for broke in the third.

STRATEGY IS THE BEST POLICY

If you have an option when asking to miss work for an OB/GYN appointment, always go to a colleague with kids: the ones with just a little bit of white gunk on the left shoulder—just a bit of crusty stuff on the lapel—these people are in the club. They get it. You may even make a positive impression on a female supervisor for leaving the office early. (Warning: Don't abuse this technique. It can really backfire. A buddy got caught coming off the golf course by a supervisor when he said he would be helping his pregnant wife into the stirrups. He got to attend all the rest of the appointments, no problem, given all his free time.)

It's also good to remember that although, to you, the birth of a child is a sacred rite requiring the attention of the known universe, your childless colleagues may not see it exactly the same way.

35

• They may wonder why they can't stay home for six weeks when their cat has kittens (no shit).
• They may wonder why they have to spend so much time covering for the breeders going to doctor appointments, squeezing out pups, staying home with the snot noses, or off playing Santa Claus.
• And they may have a point.

Try to be sympathetic to your coworkers' point of view. Ten years ago, did you want kids? Did you want to spend a great deal of time covering for those who did? Why does someone deserve special treatment, even benefits, at work just because they have kids at home? The more you get that your childless colleagues may be feeling this way, the less likely you are to piss them off by being entitled. And the more likely you are to get your ass bailed out when the doctor orders another test, and you're running just a bit late, and would you mind Bill/Judy/whoever just watching the front for a few minutes more?

FUTURE CLOUDS AND RADAR:
DOPPLER AND ULTRASOUND/SONOGRAM

A couple of tests that take place in the OB/GYN's office involve futuristic medical gear. Get ready to be amazed: Beyond the gear, you're going to be getting your first sounds and sights of your future offspring.

DOPPLER EFFECTS

The Doppler has nothing to do with the seven-day forecast. As early as eight weeks' gestation, the doc can use this small Mr. Microphone–looking device to eavesdrop on the baby's heartbeat. This test is likely to happen at one of the mom's first appointments, and is not to be missed. The fluttering sound (around 125 beats per minute is normal, but the range can vary) sounds a little like an AM broadcast from the surface of Mars, but you will never forget it. If the whole idea of being a father—having created a new life—hasn't yet sunk in, this test will close the deal for you. There he or she is. It just gets more and more real from there.

ULTRASOUNDS ARE CREEPY

Ultrasound (a.k.a. sonogram) tests will usually be prescribed by the doc starting at appointments scheduled around 12 to 14 weeks of gestation. Sometimes these sessions will happen in the doc's office and may become a regular part of exams, especially in the third trimester. In some cases you may be asked to go to a clinic with the serious high-end machines. When ultrasound is performed in the doctor's office, the gizmo is about the size of your college fridge, with lots of buttons and an eight-inch black-and-white monitor perched on top.

1.   The nurse wheels the thing in, pulls up the mom's gown, and squishes conductive clear jelly all over her stomach—which seems sort of personal and forward, but you're probably over all that at this point.

2.   The nurse will manipulate a microphone/garden hose diffuser–looking thingy over the mom's lower abdomen, bouncing high-frequency sound waves off the contents.

3.   The grainy image that results has some things in common with an X-ray, but 3-D and underwater: Hard structures like bones show up very clearly, with shadows of soft tissues also visible. It takes a while to get oriented, but pretty quickly you will get used to what you are seeing.

4.   The nurse will take measurements of the skull and thighbone, which will help determine a more accurate due date. Along the way, the nurse may print screenshots as keepsakes for the prospective parents.

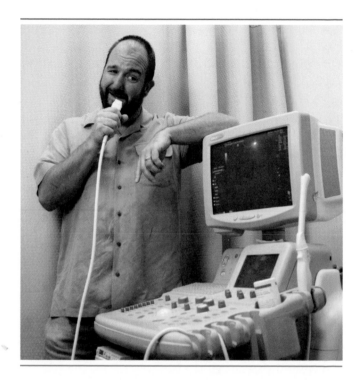

While gazing on these images of the baby's "face," it may occur to you that your wife is going to give birth to an alien. With prominent eye sockets and oversize noodle, this is not the most flattering shot you will ever see of your youngster.

BE AWARE: It's important that, if you and the mom don't want to know the sex of the child, you communicate this clearly and often to whoever sits down at the machine. If not knowing is important, you need to be persistent and repeat yourself often. Also heed warnings not to look at the screen when prompted. Once you're oriented to the picture, it doesn't take years of training to identify a twig and berries. It is easy to make an unwitting ID if you aren't careful.

TESTING, TESTING

Expecting is a time of intense optimism and looking forward to the future. But it's also a time of lurking anxieties and fears, founded and unfounded, about what might go wrong. Nothing brings these anxieties to the surface more than the prenatal testing most couples undergo. The triple or quad screenings for Down syndrome and other congenital abnormalities, usually performed between 16 and 18 weeks, are particularly stress-inducing. You're going to worry about it. She's going to worry about it. We worried about it. The numbers are in your favor, but you are still going to worry about it. The best you can do is provide each other with distractions as you wait for the results. Welcome to the world of parenting.

CARE FOR SOME FRIES WITH THAT ULTRASOUND?

Evidence that the entrepreneurial spirit is alive and well: ultrasound "booths" at your local shopping mall. Advances in 3-D ultrasound imaging led some enterprising folks to come up with a great idea: We'll sell sweet in-utero pics to pregnant moms and the dads who are willing to pay for anything to keep them happy. Ultrasound is a widely used procedure, and the medical community generally agrees that the risks are outweighed by the rewards, but it's not for glossy eight-by-tens. Tissues are heated by the application of ultrasound, and some complications have been observed in animals. In the U.S., the Food and Drug Administration suggests that couples should avoid recreational ultrasound undertaken for keepsakes.

Besides that, the blobby yellowish images produced by the 3-D ultrasound are hideously ugly, likely to horrify your friends and family. You'll have plenty of time to have Kodak moments with the kid after he or she is born. Go with the FDA on this one.

CHAPTER 3

WHY SHE'S PISSED

SYMPTOMS AND VOCAB

We are anxiously awaiting the release of a pregnancy guide for women that will let them know what to expect at any given minute of pregnancy. We have no doubt that *Your Pregnancy: Every Single Second Is Super Significant* would sell millions of copies. Many women have a seemingly insatiable appetite for information about their pregnancies—perhaps not all that surprising given the miraculous thing going on inside them.

WHAT TO EXPECT WHEN EXPECTING A CHAPTER ON PREGNANCY SYMPTOMS

All this information-seeking can be a double-edged sword, however. Reading about symptoms and milestones can spike anxiety. You may soon start to wince every time she picks up her three-inch-thick pregnancy manual because you know a mood crater/round of "suggestions" for your personal improvement is racked up and ready for launch. But short of hiding all the pregnancy books, there isn't much to be done here. Moms, especially first-timers, need frequent reassurance that what they are experiencing is normal, and that the baby is safe and progressing.

BE WARNED: She expects you to be just as interested (and you may well be). Reading this book is a step in the right direction. There is much about pregnancy that is genuinely fascinating, but our decidedly unscientific polls have revealed to us that many dads want to know just enough not to get in trouble with their spouses. So that is the goal of this chapter. We're not going to take an exhaustive look at every step of development and every symptom she will experience. (For those of you who get into the details of pregnancy, we have suggested further readings on Dad-Labs.com.) We don't need to write that book because you almost certainly have it in your house already.

Rather, we offer a modest list of what *you* can expect when she's expecting.

SYMPTOM	1ST TRIMESTER	2D TRIMESTER	3D TRIMESTER
Puking/nausea	Big-time	eases off	rare
Enlarged/ sore boobs	Yay!	Yowsa	WOW!
Constant need to pee	Going	going	going again
Tired	Pooped	drooping	dragging
Food cravings/ aversions	Strange snacks	stock up	lock on fridge
Increased sex drive	Fingers crossed	most likely	use caution
Decreased sex drive	Possible	least likely	PG-13
Emotional volatility	She's right	you're wrong	duck
Headaches	Ouch	ow	ouch-ow-ouch
Winded	Yes	more	most
Aching back	Not usually	twinges	needs daily massage
Swelling ankles/ legs	Nope	shoes still fit	flip-flop time
Indigestion/ heartburn/gas	Not so bad	pull her finger	it burns!

43

THE PREGNANCY WAGON ROLLS INTO TOWN:

ALL ABOARD?

The first and most immediate lifestyle change your partner will make is to quit drinking and/or smoking and/or using recreational drugs. You need to do whatever you can to support this effort, as these activities can lead to some serious complications, from low birth weight to fetal alcohol syndrome. Serious stuff. So it's very important that you support your wife as she zeroes out her drinking and smoking.

The obvious question is:

• *Does this mean you are obligated to quit smoking, too?*
Yes. The trouble with smoking is second-hand smoke. If you are smoking in the house, the baby will be born with nicotine onboard. Second-hand smoke in the house with a baby is a bad idea. Studies show that the carcinogenic chemicals in cigarettes move from mother to baby, whether Mom is the smoker or not. Smoking is one of the toughest addictions to crack, but will you ever have a better motivation?

• *Do you have to quit drinking, too?*
Your partner can't get second-hand drunk, so what is the clear and present danger? The issue here is largely about empathy and symbolism. From a solidarity standpoint, common sense dictates that some sacrifice—at least the appearance of standing together—is called for. So what are the options?

1. *Nine-Month Abstinence*

If this notion strikes terror into your heart, then it may actually be a good plan for you. The upside here is that you may enjoy improved health and weight loss. The downside: Improved health and weight loss may actually counteract the positive aspects of this empathetic gesture (i.e., your newly buff self will make for an annoying contrast to your wife's burgeoning belly). In addition, the mellowing effects of moderate alcohol usage have been found to be therapeutic when dealing with an individual suffering from the effects of pregnancy hormones.

2. *Drinking, But Only Away from Your Wife*

The upside of this plan is that you are obviously showing some empathy for your partner, demonstrating that you respect what she is going through, not putting it in her face that you can still drink. The downside is that your spouse may suspect every time you go out for a newspaper that you are out partying with your hair on fire. This approach requires plenty of trust and goodwill.

3. *Drinking More or Less Like You Did Before Pregnancy*

Some women will think it ridiculous that a man would quit drinking just because his wife or partner is pregnant. These women might say things like, "At least one of us should be able to drink. What's the big deal?" God bless these women. Do not abuse their gift by making "full-time designated driver" jokes. These are stupid and should not be said out loud.

When you go out with her, remember that she may get tired early and want to go home. Be cool with that. You may also want to remember that you're not as funny when your wife is sober. And remember moderation, too, because facing a hormone-fueled wife with a hangover . . . Well, that can get ugly.

PREGNANCY:
IT'S CATCHING

For some guys, pregnancy symptoms can be much more than abstract. The medical community refers to the phenomenon of men experiencing pregnancy side effects as "sympathetic pregnancy" or "Couvade," from the French for "to hatch." You may be tempted to ask if the man's symptoms include urges to get a facial or down a Cosmo, but food cravings, weight gain, and morning sickness are not all that funny. Especially on a dude.

Just how common is Couvade syndrome? Debatable. Is there a cure? Yes: It's called birth.

YOUR NEWLY PREGNANT BODY

Some men actually elect to undergo some pregnancy symptoms in order to better understand what their pregnant partners are going through. To do this they don one of several pregnancy simulation suits on the market. The Empathy Belly uses water and lead weights to re-create not only the heft of the growing baby, but also his or her movement. It comes complete with a breath constrictor to simulate the loss of lung capacity, a special bag of lead shot to press on the bladder to create urgent urination, and ample falsies. These units are pricey, but you may be able to take a demo ride from a local pregnancy educator.

But really, what kind of idiot would spend days in such a contraption, just to understand what women go through? DadLabs' own Owen Egerton, that's who. Having logged dozens of hours of self-inflicted pregnancy in a thirty-five-pound simulator for his "Prego Man" series on DadLabs.com, Owen reflects on his experiences with male pregnancy.

DAD RANT

DADDY OWEN

The plan was simple: Make a man experience pregnancy for twenty-four hours. I was chosen among the DadLabs dads for my empathic skills and adventurous spirit—plus the other guys are stronger than me.

To make the experiment a success, we invested in an Empathy Belly: thirty-five pounds of metal, sand, and water. With a bloated water belly filled with lead balls to simulate a baby's kicks, a heavy sand bag pressed against my bladder, and straps wrapped around my chest to constrict my breathing, the whole thing made me feel thick into my third trimester. But it didn't stop with the suit. Pregnant women often complain of swollen feet and morning sickness, so I was given shoes two sizes too small and a healthy dose of Ipecac.

All this, and no beer. Pregnancy can really suck.

For twenty-four hours I lived the life of a pregnant man: I slept horribly, I threw up, I had trouble getting through doors, I had to be the designated driver on a night on the town—all while toting a faux-baby in my protruding belly.

What did I learn?

1. It takes a lot of work to build another human inside your body. Having your own body expand and reconfigure affects every part of your day. There was never a moment, not even while sleeping, when I forgot my fake love child. And if I was even tempted to forget, the effort of using a toilet, climbing out of a car, or reaching for a glass quickly reminded me of my condition. I have a new admiration for the wonderful, and wonderfully challenging, journey of pregnancy.

2. There's something kind of sweet about the struggle.
By the time a child is born, the mother and baby have been through a hell of a lot together. They've had new hormones playing hopscotch with their brains, they've shared meals, they've both experienced the feeling of becoming increasingly larger in a limited space. They have tracked a nine-month marathon together, and I can only guess that a certain intimate commiseration develops.

At the stroke of hour 25, I gladly removed my pinching shoes, stripped off my Empathy Suit, and popped open a beer. I was giddy to be a non-pregnant male again. But as I leaned back comfortably, sipping my second beer, I missed the constant presence of my unborn pseudo-fetus . . . maybe just a little.

PLASTIC SURGERY:
HAVING YOUR BPA REMOVED

As an expecting and new parent, one change you may notice is that you become much more vulnerable to the health scares that erupt regularly in the media. Eventually you may find yourself lunging at the television most mornings to keep from hearing the latest issue "concerning" parents nationwide. Over time, you will learn how to sort through the facts, how to research the stories to get to the truth, and how best to take action when hysteria has some basis.

At DadLabs, one particular news scare got our attention: The chemical Bisphenol A or BPA was reported to be linked to increased childhood obesity and early onset puberty in girls. When the National Institutes of Health and the FDA start throwing around warnings, it's time to take notice.

Bisphenol A is a high-production volume chemical used in the manufacture of epoxy resins, polycarbonate plastics, and flame retardants. Polycarbonate plastics are used in food and drink packaging (particularly #7 plastics); resins are used as lacquers to coat metal products such as food cans, bottle tops, and water supply pipes. So it's everywhere.

Researchers suspect that Bisphenol A may be acting as an endocrine disruptor, exhibiting biological effects similar to those of estrogen and other hormones. In lab animals, prenatal or early exposure to these substances causes the formation of additional fat cells and predisposes the animals to obesity for life. Scientists suggest that exposure to BPA has the greatest impact on developing fetuses and children under the age of two, so it makes sense to start lowering your wife's exposure as soon as she becomes pregnant, or even before.

1. Avoid polycarbonate plastics (hard, clear plastics), especially in food and drink packaging, storage, or preparation. Most will be labeled with the triangular recycling symbol with a number 7 in the center. (Plastics #1, 2, and 5 are not as hazardous.)

2. Use glass, porcelain, or stainless cookware and dinnerware.

3. Never heat any food in plastic packaging.

4. Check water bottles to ensure they are not plastic #7s.

5. Shop for BPA-free products.

Keep your BPA-reducing techniques in mind when you start tricking out the nursery and baby-fortifying the kitchen. BPA-free bottles are a must. Okay, we'll take off the tinfoil hats now.

BEWARE THE PASSIVES (PASVS)

Now here's another side effect of pregnancy you might not expect: Being pregnant actually causes symptoms in many of the people around you, including complete strangers. Upon encountering a pregnant woman, many ordinarily self-possessed individuals will be overcome with a desire to share opinions on any and all subjects pertaining to pregnancy. In fact, nothing screams "please serve up your nuggets of prenatal wisdom, oh Random Person" more than a pregnant woman.

We have identified several categories of PASVs (Pregnancy Advice Super Villains):

1. *PASV #1: The Feeler*

Characteristics and habitat: Presents in both male and female varieties; this passive can be found in almost any coffee shop or whole foods store. You'll know you are facing a Feeler when a total stranger touches your wife's stomach.

Unsolicited advice: Will tend to advocate for whole/organic foods and yoga.

Action: Be prepared for the Feeler to critique the contents of your shopping cart. Be prepared to insert yourself bodily between your wife's belly and the Feeler's groping hand.

2. *PASV #2: The Pseudo-Doc*

Characteristics and habitat: Primarily male, Pseudo-Docs are found most frequently in pharmacy prescription waiting areas, airline terminals, and chain bookstores. The PD has at his disposal an enormous treasure trove of health information, despite having no actual medical training whatsoever.

Unsolicited advice: Will in all likelihood be based on "studies" the PD has read. Will generally include prenatal vitamin recs, warnings regarding toxicity in household cleaners, etc.

Action: Be absolutely certain not to mention BPAs unless you have the afternoon free.

3. *PASV #3: The Horror Show*

Characteristics and habitat: Both male and female, found mostly at dinner parties or anywhere the drinks flow freely. Born without tact, with their boundaries washed away in a sea of white wine, these creatures feed on your darkest fears.

Unsolicited advice: Not really advice so much as intensely graphic accounts of the darkest imaginable labor and delivery moments. Particular focus given to hemorrhoid tales and episiotomy narratives.

Action: Horror shows are easily diverted onto non-pregnancy-related yet disgusting topics. Ask about hernias, airline travel, or septic systems.

4. *PASV #4: Your Mom*
Characteristics and habitat: She may mean well, and may only wish to help you and your partner benefit from her years of experience, but advice from this PASV can really wreak havoc. She is most likely to speak up in closed and moving vehicles, during mealtimes, and under any circumstance when escape is impossible.

Unsolicited advice: Covers pretty much any and all topics.

Action: Keep your mom very busy on projects that are forward looking. And ask her to drive herself for a few months.

Ordinarily, your partner might deal with this random kind of input with a shrug and a tart "whatever." But pregnancy can act like kryptonite, lowering the pregnant mom's otherwise formidable powers of defense. What's a dad to do?

- Deploy your powers in buffering, deflecting, and soothing.
- Get the advice-giver to speak to you instead of to your wife.
- Change the subject to something other than the pregnancy. Or, if you arrive on the scene too late, listen carefully in the aftermath and reassure your partner that she is doing everything just fine.
- Be very careful about taking advice from non-professional, untrained, and/or uncertified sources. This book excepted, of course.

WHAT WE LEARNED IN BIRTHING CLASS

You are not pregnant. You will not give birth to the baby. In fact, your role in the whole process of labor and delivery is pretty peripheral, at best. Now, the last thing we would want to do is to seem cynical about a man's role in the birthing process, but it is also fairly easy to overplay what a man's place in the delivery room really is. Let's be realistic:

- As a birth consultant, you lack the crucial skill set.
- As a labor and delivery coach, your experience is limited by your reproductive organs.
- You can and should be helpful, empathetic, and supportive, but a key player, you are not.

Does this mean that birth classes are a waste of your time? It doesn't really matter, because you're not getting out of it. At the point in the second trimester when your partner asks, "Honey, what kind of birthing class do you want to take?" your response will not be, "There's more than one kind?" or "Why go to the class if I'll never take the exam?" Nor will you offer to paint the house instead.

You'll go because nothing is more democratic than a birthing class. After all, there aren't any forms to fill out to get pregnant—there's no screening process, no membership requirements, no minimums, no union. We all have babies, and we all come together to worry about it at birthing class.

- You'll get a look at all kinds of dads and quickly realize that you are neither the most on top of it nor the biggest doofus in the history of fatherhood.

- The characters in the class as well as the subject matter will give you and your partner a great deal to talk about.

- And talking about the subject of the pregnancy is the best way to show your support and make the pregnant mom more comfortable.

Choosing which class to attend is a lot like registration at college: the teacher is more important than the course. So throw out an e-mail blast and ask your friends and male colleagues if they had a teacher they liked (or if there is a teacher to avoid). An instructor with a sense of humor can make all the difference.

There are two popular schools of birthing classes: Lamaze, which emphasizes breathing and pain management, and Bradley, which emphasizes the father's role in coaching. Both methods offer classes that stick close to the party line. In the end, there really isn't all that much difference between them:

- Both enable the husband to feel like he has an active role in the delivery—which can really help during crunch time.

- Both employ crappy instructional videos.

- Both will help you clue into the lingo flying around the delivery room.

We tend to like the independent birthing instructor who can pick and choose from the various methods without getting too orthodox. The important thing is that you'll be thinking about and talking about the pregnancy with your partner. You may even pick up a technique or two that will make your wife more comfortable during pregnancy or labor.

PICKING YOUR NAMES

As with most issues surrounding pregnancy, it's important for the expecting dad to let Mom know that he's interested and engaged in important decisions. Picking the name your child will carry around with her for the rest of her life probably ranks as one of the most important, and it's a lock to provide hours of feisty but fun give-and-take during the second and third trimesters—when light banter can be hard to come by.

It can also prove frustrating. So many possibilities! Then you both have to agree on one. What if she likes Irving and you like Ishmael?

1. Get a special notebook: It will make for a fun keepsake, and you might want to refer to it when baby number two comes along.

2. Sit down with your wife to compile the list. Remember, these conversations should be fun. Keep it light.

3. Start with family names. Jot down your parents', grandparents', and your own names of course. Got a rich uncle named Buford Smallpuckey? Put him on the list. He just may find the gesture appealing enough to redo his will.

4. Peruse baby name resources. The library or bookstore might be a good next stop. There are a slew of books and Web sites that offer lists of names, name meanings, and even charts and graphs of name popularity. Add your favorites to the list without being too picky at this point.

5. Get creative. Now peruse the shelves for books that were particularly meaningful to you. Characters and authors have cool

names. The same goes for your favorite movies, TV shows, and sports teams. Who were your heroes? Put 'em down.

6. Consider middle names. The nice thing about first and middle names is you can mix it up a little: One from the family, one from the Web. Explaining the provenance of the names, and engaging the kids in a little family history, is well worth the annoyance of an old-timey middle name. Start trying out combinations to see how they sound together—and how they sound with the baby's last name, of course.

7. Keep your options open. Once couples get a short list, they may stop there, waiting to meet the baby before making a final decision.

THE NAME TEST

At DadLabs we like to take the names out for a little test drive. Any thorough name testing here at the Labs includes three stages: the Handshake test, the Holler test, and the Pre-K shakedown test.

1. Handshake Test
Put her out there, pump the hand, and introduce yourself like an insurance salesman. "Hey, there, I'm [insert favorite name here]. Nice to meet you." Try it out 5 to 10 times, imagining a variety of situations: prom date, meeting parents, job interview, mortgage broker meeting, big conference. What does the name inspire?

2. Holler Test
Go to a field or abandoned building and scream the full name a number of times. Try anticipating parental exhortations such as: "[Insert full name]! Come here right now!" "[Insert full name]!

Stop pestering your sister." "[Insert full name]! Leave that nice man alone." "[Insert full name]! Go talk to your mother."

3. Pre-K Shakedown Test

Do your immature worst with the proposed name. How can you twist it, tease it, or make it sound like a bodily function? How will that clever fourth-grade bully turn the name against your progeny? Almost any name can be used to tease, but are you making it too easy? Let your sophomoric imagination be your guide.

THE MOST IMPORTANT ADVICE ABOUT NAMES

However you come to decide on your name or names, keep them under your hat. Do not poll parents or in-laws beforehand. Make this important decision with your wife alone, and wait to announce it until the baby is in your arms.

TEN THINGS NEVER TO SAY TO YOUR PREGNANT PARTNER

10. Is that on your Best Odds diet?
9. You're not nearly as big as [insert neighbor's name] got.
8. Don't be irrational.
7. I need my rest, too.
6. Having a designated driver ROCKS HARD!
5. That's the hormones talking.
4. What about me?
3. So, the boobs . . . Here to stay?
2. Mmmmm. Oysters.
1. Jeez, I'm so glad I'm not a woman.

CHAPTER 4

BABY POWDER FOR YOUR BOTTOM LINE

BABYPROOFING YOUR FINANCES

If you've heard it once, you've heard it a million times: Kids are expensive.

Actually, that part is true. Kids *are* expensive.

The myth is that kids are expensive because of shoes. Well, that part is also true: Shoes are expensive, but not nearly as expensive as such items as medical and insurance costs, childcare, and yes—you already have to worry about college.

Dad, you need to babyproof your finances.

Think of it this way. You and the expecting mom are partners in a family business; let's call it Me & Maw, Inc. (NASD: PAMA). You made it through the startup phase and have achieved financial stability; now it's time to expand operations. Actually, your partner has been expanding for quite some time, but that's another chapter. Expansion requires significant financial resources. You must acquire new capital items, adequately support your new employee, and finally devise and implement a long-term corporate strategy.

It's time to make a plan.

CAPITAL EXPENDITURE:
PRE-LAUNCH

Your new employee is a pretty special hire, tops in her birth class, super smart, a real self-starter. It makes good business sense to do all you can to take special care of this new member of the team. First step is to outfit a fancy office and cushy employee break room. Here is a list of the basic baby items and some comparable costs in man currency:

Car Seat • Bassinet • Stroller • Changing Table • Crib • Diaper Pail • Diaper Bag • Breast Pump

ME & MAW, INC.

CMO
[MOMMY]

**VALUED
EMPLOYEE**
[BABY]

CDO
[DADDY]

Total Man Cost: On the low end, about the same as a brand-name 32-inch HDTV and on the high end as much as a top-of-the-line 52-inch plasma HDTV complete with the Home Theater Surround Sound package.

As you can see, even conservative to moderate capital expenditures will set you back some significant coin, and if you want to pamper your new employee like an early '90s Internet startup, get out your wallet, because high-end baby crapola gets pricey.

And the kid's not even here yet.

Financial note: Although capital spending may seem hefty, especially since the new hire has not done a day of work yet, remember that there are investors out there willing to jump in and ease your financial burden. Once you go public and let everyone know you are expanding operations, it is time to have a corporate party (a.k.a. a baby shower). We'll give you more information on showers later, but note here that showering is a great way to acquire many of the essentials your company needs and positively affects your bottom line.

OPERATING COSTS:
SHORT TERM

With capital infrastructure in place, your focus should turn to daily operations. During the first few months of life your new employee will essentially eat, poop, cry, and sleep.

The comparable costs projected here are averages and will vary from company to company. Let's face it: Some corporations buy a brand-new fleet of European sports cars every year for upper management, and other CEOs still drive the 1972 El Camino with the green vinyl interior that Uncle Dave gave them twenty years ago. The point is these projections are ballpark figures that will help you identify your new operating expenses depending on your taste and budget. So plan accordingly.

MEALS

DadLabs highly recommends breastfeeding, not only because it is the best thing for Mom and baby, but because breastfeeding will save you a good deal of cash! We suggest that you invest in a sturdy, dependable breast pump and use formula as a supplement as needed. The reduction in your monthly formula bill will quickly pay for the initial cash investment in the pump.

However, some new Chief Mommy Officers (CMOs) find breastfeeding very difficult, and a few find it impossible for numerous reasons. Thus, our projections for meal expense assume a first-year diet exclusively composed of formula. New babies eat every two to three hours, and although it looks like lemon-lime Kool-Aid, baby formula is much more expensive.

Projected First-Year Man Cost: About the same as a top-of-the-line 42,000 BTU gas barbecue grill.

POLLUTION ABATEMENT

Your new little employee is much like a small coal-fired power plant. You supply the resources in the form of breast milk and formula, and in return you get energy in the form of crying, spitting up, and eventually cooing and smiling. This production process creates emissions called "poop." Given the new environmental standards in place due to global warming, you are required to install an emission abatement system more commonly known as diapers and wipes. Most new babies emit 8 to 12 times a day, and a diaper on average costs about the same as one play on an old-school arcade game. Although the frequency of emissions decreases as the first year of employment moves along, you should be prepared to abate for several years.

Projected First-Year Man Cost: Comparable to a new set of cavity-back Ping Irons.

HUMAN RESOURCES

The National Labor Relations Baby Board established a list of requirements that all employers are responsible for providing to nonexempt employees during the first year of their working life.

Baby Labor Law 31, Section 4233, Volume 69, Paragraph 24 states: "Each new employee break room must be furnished with the following: age-appropriate clothing,* age-appropriate developmental toys, infant tub, bath towels, baby nail clippers, teething rings, pacifiers, baby thermometer, baby monitor, fever reducer, soap, butt paste, burp cloths, bibs, multiple onesies, and multiple sets of sometimes needless items that Mom decides to purchase."

Projected First-Year Man Cost: The same as two front row tickets to a Rolling Stones concert.

*Financial note: Most CMOs love to buy super-cute clothing for the little ones, so make sure to set a reasonable budget before the new employee arrives. Trust us, it sucks to drop a C-note for an outfit that is only going to be worn and puked on twice.

PROFESSIONAL DEVELOPMENT

In addition to running Me & Maw, Inc., you and your partner may actually have real jobs. More and more couples today feature two careers. Be advised that the CMO will want to spend as much time with the infant as possible. In the United Sates, federal law mandates that companies offer parents at least twelve weeks of family leave immediately following the birth of a child. That number is fifty-two weeks in the UK and a whopping sixteen months in Sweden. Dads are allowed to take a small portion of this time, but the majority of leave is reserved for Mom, except in Sweden, where time is equally split between Mom and Dad. (Go Swedes!) If your family boasts two working parents, ultimately both you and Mom will go back to work, so you must contend with procuring childcare.

Quality childcare is both expensive and difficult to find. Waiting lists form several months to a year in advance, so make your reservations early even if you are not sure whether you will need the care. As you shop around, consider:

- Do you have a good rapport with the staff?
- Do you like the facility?
- What is the proximity to your home or place of work?
- Does the daily program mesh with your daily work schedule?
- Does the yearly schedule jibe with your vacation schedule?
- Does the program offer extended toddler care as well?

If one parent is going to stay home full-time with the new employee, look into part-time mother's or father's day out-programs. Childcare is tough, and you may need a break.

The price of childcare varies widely, from five hundred to several thousand dollars a month, depending on the type of program. Our projections are based on reasonably priced, private, full-day programs that follow the typical school calendar.

Projected First-Year Man Cost: Almost as much as a new 1200 cc Harley Davidson Sportster.

Financial note: Conduct a cost-benefit analysis when deciding whether to seek childcare. Consider how much the least-paid parent actually brings home after taxes and compare this to the out-of-pocket expense for childcare. There may not be as big of a gap as you imagined. Couple this with the luxury of getting to spend the majority of your time with your child during that precious first year of life, and staying home just may be the best option.

DIRECT MEDICAL

The final line item in your baby-operating budget that will significantly affect your monthly P&L is medical expense. The amount
you shell out is largely dependent on what services are covered
by insurance or other health care programs, but you should be
prepared to shoulder some out-of-pocket expense each month during that first year. If you live in Europe or have a progressive U.S.
policy that covers infants' "milestone" and "well care" checkups,
your outlay is likely to be minimal, but if you live in Toledo and
have a high deductible and co-pay policy, budget at least enough
to cover two cases of beer and a bucket of hot wings a month to
care for the little nipper.

Projected First-Year Man Cost: About the same as a midlevel
digital SLR camera.

So there you have it. Your direct operating expenses are likely
to increase roughly as much as it would cost you to purchase a
brand-new high-end jet ski in the first year alone. Now is the time
to sit down and work out your first-year budget. Have an upper-
level management meeting with the CMO and make sure you are
on the same page concerning your financial priorities. It is better to have these conversations in the relative calm of pregnancy
(say, in the second trimester) than to wait until the new hire
starts, when you both may be just a little tired.

Capital infrastructure is going to cost you more than a good
set of golf clubs; that first-year operating increase may set you
back as much as a week at an exclusive beach resort in the
Caribbean; and over the long term you are going to drop a freaking bundle. And since you are the big dog, the financial burden
rests squarely on your shoulders. But always remember the bottom line: It's not about the money; it's about being a Dad!

CHAPTER 5

GEARING UP FOR BABY

NESTING FOR MEN

Somewhere in your house do you have a room? A study or a den? A place that's yours, where you keep your guy stuff? Well kiss it goodbye, because here comes the babyjunk.

Just remember: You may be losing some real estate, but it's a great time to earn some brownie points. Setting up the nursery and getting the house ready for the baby allow you to kick it into high gear. In this chapter, we'll look at the basic purchases for newborns as well as the more advanced tricks of the trade for babyproofing your home once the little one gets to be mobile.

Although it may seem early, start thinking about the nursery when the pregnancy hits around 30 weeks. (Just in case you haven't learned to speak in weeks, "30 weeks" translates as "two to three months before the baby is due.") The biggest reason to start planning is that your baby might come prematurely. Other circumstances in your life also might change unexpectedly, like your work or the health of your parents. Our best advice is to be prepared. Before you bring home the baby, you'll want to have a car seat, a crib, a changing table, diapers, wipes, and a diaper pail.

THE CAR SEAT

We start with the car seat because you will need one to get home from the hospital. There are three types:

- *Infant:* The type your kid will use for about one year or until outgrowing the weight and height limits for the seat.
- *Child:* Once your child outgrows the infant seat, you can use this until the kid is about 40 pounds, depending on the manufacturer's specifications.
- *Booster:* The type you use until your kid is ready to use a regular seatbelt. (Dude, that's eons away.)

For those of you keeping track, you are about to enter the infant phase. Here are the basic things you should look for:

1 Comfort features.

Many reviews leave out this fact, but your kid will be sitting (actually lying) in this piece of plastic for many hours to come, and a comfortable kid is one who might not cry. Comfort is achieved through padding as well as designs that isolate the straps that ride beneath the padding. Pop up the hood—actually lift off the upholstery—and see what kind of padding is underneath. Don't worry about tearing up the upholstery, since these pieces of fabric are made to come out and be washable. And from poop leaks to spit-up, you *will* be washing them.

2. Base unit.

Most infant car seats come with a base unit that stays in the car. The actual seat, which is really a kind of bed, then attaches to and detaches from the base unit. This is not a gimmick to get you to buy more gear. Infants are often lulled to sleep by riding in a car, so you will want to be able to extract the baby from the car without unbuckling her and waking her up once you get to your destination. Also, the portability of the car seat allows you to take the baby wherever you go even if she is not asleep. (Hint: Go to as many restaurants as you can until she starts crawling.) Having an extra base unit for your second car is super helpful and is worth the additional expense. Some strollers are designed to fit a car seat as well. (More to come on strollers shortly.)

3. Head restraint.

Your kid's head and neck will be about as stable as a wet noodle for a while. That's why you are taught to always support a newborn baby's head when holding it. Many car seats come with a head support that keeps your child's noggin from moving around too much.

4. Sunshade.

A good sunshade can also help your child sleep. But not all sunshades are created equal. A great sunshade can cover the baby from any angle of the sun, folds easily, and is not super bulky when retracted. Try before you buy.

5. Buckles.

You will buckle and unbuckle your kids thousands of times in the next five years. Check out the straps on the car seat to see if they are easy to do and undo—and most important of all, whether the straps are prone to tangle easily. Several manufacturers have developed straps with "memory" so that your optimal tension settings do not require readjusting every time you buckle the little one into the seat. (See page 128 for further information.)

THE BASSINET

Your kid will probably not even sleep in a crib right away but instead sleep for a few hours at a time in a mini crib called a bassinet. The bassinet goes right in your bedroom for the first few weeks, when the baby is eating every couple of hours around the clock. It's handy for Mom and reassuring for everybody involved. Bassinets are so temporary that it might be best to borrow one. Just be sure the equipment is up-to-date for safety standards.

THE CRIB

Cribs are one of the most expensive items found in the nursery. Before you pay a lot for the right designer or feature-filled model, ask yourself: Do you remember yours? Probably not—so don't fret too much about this purchase.

Consider:

• How easy is it to raise and lower the side walls of the crib?
• Does it come with wheels?
• Does it have extra storage underneath (for spare sheets and blankets)?
• Is the crib adjustable in height so that, as the baby gets bigger and can stand up in the crib, you can lower the mattress level?
• Does it convert into a child's bed?
• Does it come with a mattress?
• Is it safety rated?

You might be tempted to get a used crib, but be careful, especially if the crib is a family heirloom made before 1974. Safety rules for cribs—specifying, among other things, the safest width between slats—were not in place before that time.

If you buy a crib that was shipped flat-boxed, then you are going to have to assemble it. Which is a bummer since many crib designers have yet to attend the IKEA college of simple design. What makes it even more difficult is that cribs are not bookshelves. They have moving parts, drawers, safety mechanisms, and more. Be prepared to spend a little time putting your crib together.

CRIB ALTERNATIVES

Many families choose to sleep directly with their newborns. This is called "co-sleeping" or "family bed." Although some parents adopt the practice for bonding reasons, it also has the practical benefit of facilitating late-night nursing, since the baby is right by your side. Just be aware: Co-sleeping will put a serious crimp in your ability to sleep. And as for its affecting your sex life: moot point.

One big worry about sleeping with your baby will be smothering and smooshing him. There are bassinets and other contraptions specially developed to go in or beside the bed to allow the kid to sleep near you but not in your rollover zone.

Helpful tip: Put an adult bed in the nursery. That way, whoever is taking care of the baby can sleep there and let the other sleep-deprived parent catch up. (Hint: Forget it. You will never catch up.)

CRIB ACCESSORIES

Bumpers are the pads that cushion the crib slats at baby level, keeping the little one from hitting the wall in turn three. Their function, beyond aesthetics, is actually debatable, and many pediatricians recommend keeping the crib bumper-free so that baby can't get tangled in the ties securing the pads or, eventually, use them as a launching pad to crawl up and over the bars. And though pillows, stuffed animals, and toys look cute in the crib, they are no-nos: Many contain choking hazards and, according to studies, increase the risk of Sudden Infant Death Syndrome (SIDS) if the material blocks your baby's airway.

THE CHANGING TABLE

Once you have the crib set up, you need to turn to the changing table. This can be either a dedicated piece of furniture called a changing table or a chest of drawers with a soft pad mounted on top. Note that for the latter you will need to pay heed to the strap that screws into the back of the chest of drawers to keep the pad from slipping off with the baby.

The nice thing about specialty changing tables is that they are a nice height for grabbing ankles and swabbing buns, and they have lots of storage down below. You'll want room within reach for diapers, wipes, ointment, powder—the works.

Tip: Don't be tempted to put in shelves above the changing table. One oops and ouch!

DIAPERS

Cloth or disposable? Disposable is way easier, but anyone who chooses cloth will take you on with the religious fervor of an environmentalist. In real terms, valid arguments can be made on both sides regarding environmental impact (cloth diaper delivery services use fuel, which contributes pollutants, but disposables inarguably gunk up the works in a big way).

If you want to try cloth yourself, go for it, but consider hiring a diaper cleaning service rather than laundering them yourself. We have known many well-meaning parents who recycle and maybe even drive electric cars, but they finally gave in on disposable diapers. Just don't throw them on the highway.

Whatever you choose, prepare for sticker shock. You may want to consider joining a members-only price club.

WIPES

Three simple words: Buy in bulk. All wipes are pretty much equally durable and effective for getting the job done, so look for the best bargains. Helpful tip: Once you buy a pack of wipes in a plastic dispenser box, you only have to buy refills for the box.

DIAPER PAIL

Make sure you get a diaper pail with some kind of sphincter thingy that closes the bag and doesn't let the stink out. This is not a job for your kitchen trash can. Parents are religious about diaper pails, so ask anyone who is still in the diaper phase for recommendations. The truth of the matter is, however, that you will always have a little stink in the air. (Welcome to parenthood.) Look for models that have a hefty capacity but still fit easily into the diaper changing area.

MISCELLANEOUS ITEMS

Finally, there are the items that are certainly nice to have on hand once the baby is born, but are by no means the things you need to run out and buy right away.

• *Baby tub:* A baby tub can be rather handy, and is safest for baby, but the kitchen sink will also do the trick.

• *Glider/rocker:* Like you really need to spend money on a special rocker for nursing. But if you can afford it, it just might save your marriage or partnership. Nothing is better for helping to lull a baby to sleep at night. If you have a colicky baby, chances are you will buy one of these no matter what your income. The best gliders have a matching ottoman that makes it even more of a pleasure for Mom.

• *Digital camera:* Little hand-held still cameras have come a long way in the last five years. They also take great movies. Their size makes them super convenient to throw in the diaper bag. If you are in the least bit a photo buff, mortgage the farm and get a digital SLR camera. The big kind. Your kid will give endless opportunities to use it, and no parent regrets having great pix of his kids.

• *Bottles:* A good idea to leave this for Mom to choose among the endless varieties of nipple shapes and bottle materials. You both will want to be extra careful to choose bottles that are BPA-free (see page 50).

• *Formula:* Powdered or liquid formula is used either as a substitute for breast milk when Mom cannot produce a sufficient supply or when baby needs supplemental nutrition in addition to Mom's milk. Doctors agree that breast milk is the best thing for your baby, but when a woman cannot (take it from us, this is not a laughing matter), formula is the next best choice. Newer brands provide organic selections that contain fewer additives than standard formulas. Be prepared that formula can get pricey, especially in liquid form.

• *Breast pump:* Mom's breasts get full of milk, and if they are not fully drained when baby nurses, she runs the risk of complications (everything from blocked ducts to a more painful infection of the breast known as mastitis). On second thought, the breast pump should be on your list of must-haves as soon as you leave the hospital. Chances are, you will be able to purchase or rent one from the hospital lactation staff. Get the most powerful one you can afford. The pumped milk can be stored in the fridge or freezer,

75

ready for you or another caregiver to give to the kid. Working moms and sleepy-at-night moms really depend on them.

• *Night light:* You will be up a lot in the middle of the night, so a higher-end nightlight is a great purchase.

• *High chair:* As long as you are raking in the big dollar booty from baby showers, go ahead and plan for the future, when your baby will be sitting up and eating solids. High chairs should be easy to clean. Look for minimal nooks and crannies in the seat area as well as a tray that is easy to remove and wash. The buckles you use to secure your kid into the seat come in every variety imaginable; make sure they are easy for you to use.

BABYPROOFING 101

This moving target will change as your child grows: If you are the parent of a ten-year-old, child proofing means locking down the Internet, whereas as the parent of a newborn, you don't need to be concerned about much for at least the first couple months. But seeing as you'll soon have enough on your hands, it's a good idea to start with at least some basic babyproofing around the house:

• *Electrical outlet covers.* Cheap plastic inserts are the easiest way to protect an electrical outlet, but the inserts are tough to remove and often get lost despite your best intentions. For high-use areas, buy a spring-loaded outlet cover that slides to the side when you want to plug something in.

• *Cabinet locks.* Keep the kids out of the poison! Locks come in a variety of styles, from screw-ons to stick-ons to manual knob restrictors to magnetically triggered locks. Which ones you choose depends on personal preference and the doors or cabinets you need to secure. When in doubt, move the dangerous items

Small hazards loom large when there's a baby on the loose.

(household cleaners, paint, any sort of heavy object that can tip onto a child) to a secure spot, high out of reach.

• *Gates.* Kids can fall down stairs. Baby gates keep that from happening. There are two varieties: compression gates and screw-into-the wall gates. All compression gates will mar your walls despite their claims, as will screw-in gates. Screw-in gates are much sturdier, but require a little bit more installation on your end. Word of advice: Don't worry about the walls, they are doomed either way. The most important gates to install are at the top and bottom of any staircases. You may also want to install gates at the entryway to the kitchen and in the baby's play area, where he will spend most of his time.

• *Toliet seat locks.* Kids can drown in a toilet, but it is more likely they will deposit your cell phone there. A simple lock will deter either occurrence.

• *Bathtub safety equipment.* Once your kid starts taking baths in the bathtub proper (this won't be for a good few months to half a year), you might want to install deterrents to keep her from chipping a tooth on the faucet or playing with the hot water handle. Some devices serve as gates to keep the kid away from the faucet and controls, while others clamp onto the faucet as padding. Important tip: Turn down the temperature on your hot water heater to avoid scalding.

• *Doorknob covers.* Doorknob covers make it so that only a strong-handed adult can open a door to areas you don't want your kid to have access. Just be careful when you come home a little unsober.

• *Furniture straps.* A kid can get seriously injured by a tipping bookcase or chest of drawers. Since she will climb on furniture as she learns to stand up, it is advisable to secure such things to a wall.

• *Corner guards.* Crawl around in your house when it's dark one night and you will come away with stitches. Corner guards take the edge off pointy coffee tables by cushioning the corners. (Hint:

You might want to put away that glass-top coffee table until your child reaches adulthood.)

All of this safety equipment is easily purchased at most baby big-box stores or through online catalogs.

BUYING A STROLLER

We could devote an entire chapter just to buying a stroller. The whole experience can be pretty fun, like buying a car. Unless of course you dread buying cars. What's required is a bit of extra research into both your needs and the models that best fit with your needs.

In the early weeks, if you are an urbanite pedestrian, a convertible stroller that can take an infant or an infant car seat are most useful. The stroller in effect becomes your car. If you are living in the burbs and you drive more, you can usually get by with sticking the kid in the car seat and carrying the kid in the seat wherever you go.

But soon enough, he or she will be big enough to sit up in an actual stroller. This happens at around six months. Be forewarned that these full-on baby strollers can be pricey, so you may want to use some of your baby shower dough for financing.

The basic offerings include:

- Umbrella strollers that are generally cheap and lightweight.
- Wagon-like strollers that have storage space galore.
- High-performance strollers that have been designed by aeronautical engineers.
- Off-road strollers that work well both on the gravel walking trail and for hopping curbs.

• Running strollers for the parent who thought he or she would stay in shape.

• Hybrids strollers that offer a frame with attachments that change as the baby grows.

No matter which stroller you choose, kick the wheels, take it for a test drive, and ask the following questions:

• How easily does the stroller collapse?
• How lightweight is it?
• Are the buckles easy to use?
• Is the fabric easy to clean?
• Is there a hand brake?
• How sturdy are the wheel locks?
• Do the front or back wheels lock down for straight-ahead fast travel to the next terminal?
• How easy is it to steer?
• Does the height of the handle adjust for tall dads?
• Does it have storage?
• Does the sunshade actually do anything?
• Does it recline?

Once you've narrowed down your selection, ask your friends for their recommendations. Read up on the latest online reviews as well. The testimony of parents "in the field" is invaluable when it comes to deciding the make and model.

BUDGETING:
PURCHASING IS NOT PARENTING

Okay, we're huge hypocrites. We just told you to save for college, then handed you the bill for all this junk. Ouch! Time to do some budgeting.

- Look again at your labor and delivery costs.
- Anticipate your increased overall monthly costs.
- Figure out what you can afford to spend on setting up the nursery without going hugely into debt.

If Mom balks and wants to go on a spending spree, you can tell her that being financially responsible is being a good parent. Gently remind her that the baby probably won't even remember the crib or whether the drapes match the paint; that the baby will want her love more than a fifty-dollar mobile.

When it's time to buy, the big box stores are great for selection and price, and boutiques are great for personal service, but don't forget consignment and second-hand baby stores. Nobody uses baby stuff very hard or very long.

From the earliest moments in the baby's life, education is more important than decoration. Act accordingly. Get the essentials covered, and add on only what you can afford. Then get your friends to throw you some kick-ass baby showers.

SHOWERS FOR HIM AND HER; OR, THE BABY KEGGER

Traditionally, showers have been for women, but nowadays it is not uncommon to have couples' showers in which Dad participates. If you are part of the shower, you need some ground rules:

• No silly games like guessing Mommy's tummy size or dirty diaper party favors with chocolate pudding for poo.

• There must be almost the same number of men guests as women guests.

• There must be some sort of good food and/or beer. Mimosas work well for morning events.

Instead of a baby shower, why not have one of your best buds throw you a baby kegger? You provide the beer and throw a party. If you don't like the idea of setting up a gift registry, host an auction. Ask your funniest buddy to MC and offer up various goods and services for sale to the highest bidder. Any bids on the last round of golf with the expecting dad before his life changes forever? Got to let the motorcycle or the season tickets go? All proceeds go to the stroller fund or baby's education fund.

TOP 10 DAD-CENTRIC SHOWER/KEGGER GIFTS

1. A still-image camera that also takes movies
2. A DadGear™ Diaper Bag
3. An external hard drive for all the movies and photos the new dad will be taking

4. An iPhone (to show off pics of the baby, of course)

5. A *Due Dads Guide to Labor and Delivery* DVD

6. An alma mater onesie

7. A contribution to baby's education fund

8. A box of cigars

9. A *Raising Arizona* DVD

10. A sexy woman jumping out of a cake (just kidding, Hon)

OBSESSIVE-COMPULSIVE CLEANING

Finally, be prepared for Mom's nesting instinct to click into high gear. Getting the house ready for the baby can be a pretty crazy time for her. Remember that she is hormonal, and there are things going on in her head and body that are not going on in yours.

Some of her requests, like cleaning the grout or dusting the baseboards, may seem irrational. But strap on the rubber gloves and grab a bucket. The bigger she becomes, the harder it will be for her to do things herself. Some things that you might be asked to do include painting the nursery, painting the rooms leading to the nursery, painting the outside of the house near the nursery, and painting new numbers on the curb. You might be the one to assemble flat-packed furniture. And then rearrange it five times. Hanging pictures, rearranging the kitchen, throwing out old junk—these are all now your jobs. Get used to it, and try to enjoy it. But also remember to take some time off to just relax with your partner. Drink in your life now and what it means to be a couple: Joyful. Hopeful. Rested. And then: Sleep. Sleep. Sleep. Sleep.

CHAPTER 6

BRING CHANGE FOR THE SNACK MACHINES

OUR GREATEST DELIVERY ROOM TIPS

It's time.

Maybe her water has broken or the contractions have increased in frequency and duration. Or maybe you've scheduled a C-section. Regardless, when the time comes to get your wife to the hospital, you too might feel a rush—a deep caveman instinct that says: Male must get female to hospital. Go with it. Protect her. Drive safely. And cross your fingers that you will not have to deliver the baby in the car. We can't help you there.

If you are reading this chapter while on your way to the hospital, please put the book down and drive.

FROM CAVEMAN TO SECRET AGENT MAN

From the moment the hospital doors whoosh open to greet you and your partner, things change. She is now a patient. And there is about to be a second patient with his or her own little ankle band. Which makes you third down on the list. The provider/caveman must now let the pros take over.

Be thankful, because you are about to be witness to, and even participate in, a major procedure. There are few if any other procedures in a hospital involving surgery and bodily fluids where a partner gets to sit in, much less participate (e.g., cutting the cord). Prepare to provide assistance and support when appropriate, but leave most of the heavy lifting to the OB/GYN or midwife.

This does not mean you are off the hook. You merely have a new job as Secret Agent Man, working for the motherland, although comparing the impending new mom to a landmass is not something you will ever want to do. The Secret Agent Man, heretofore known as the expectant father, works as a first line of defense, a mediator, between the machine that is the hospital and the person who is in so much pain she can't even express it herself. More on your mission follows.

You have already chosen to accept it.

DELIVERING FOR DELIVERY

First you have to make it to the delivery room, and since your partner may not be walking at this point, it's your job to work out the necessary logistics.

● Not to worry. Just waltz in any hospital door and shout in a panicked way: "My wife is having a baby!" Or, better yet, let her scream through a contraction. You will get immediate service.

● You can also plan ahead. Many hospitals have a dedicated check-in procedure for laboring moms, be it through a special women's entrance, the emergency room, or the maternity floor. Regardless, know this ahead of time, along with how to procure a wheelchair (they should be plentiful).

● Planning ahead also means researching the hospital's parking rules. If Mom is really far along in labor, you might have to rush right into the delivery room. It may be hours before you have the desire or time to move a car.

DAD RANT

DADDY ☐☐☐ CLAY

I was totally supportive of my wife's decision to have a natural childbirth, right up to the part where she gave birth naturally. My wife was fiercely determined to be anesthesia-free for the birth of our second child, a desire fueled in part by her disappointment in the delivery of our first: prematurely and by emergency C-section. I knew I had to get behind this, even as it caused her pain.

How much pain, I had absolutely no clue. And I also had no idea that watching my wife suffer would turn me into a ranting and raving Neanderthal. With each successive contraction, the hair on my arms grew thicker, and my brow ridge became more pronounced. *Must do something to stop pain*, screamed my brainstem.

The battle took a toll on my civility. By the time she was five centimeters, I wanted to get in a fistfight with a candy striper. By the time she was seven, I dragged in a freshly killed stag. By the time she was ready to push, I was challenging the midwife to a cage match. Even as my thoughts grew more muddled and my words more monosyllabic, I kept running my mouth, to the point that my wife, her face red and her features contorted in pain, paused between contractions to remind me that she could still hear me. And could I please shut up.

Try saying some things you may have never said before:

- Honey, I love you.
- You look so beautiful.
- I am so proud to have you as the mother of our child.
- I look forward to dancing at our daughter's wedding.
- You have done such a good job in this pregnancy.

Or doing some things you might have never done before:

Caress her face • Rub her back • Give her a random, unannounced kiss • Rub her feet

There are lots of things that you probably *shouldn't* say during labor. Here are just a few of our favorites:

1. Just tough it out, honey.
2. Is that normal?
3. Back in the day, they just dropped one in the fields and kept working.
4. Well my mom said _____ (fill in the blank).
5. Why the hell is birth on the metric system?
6. I am so glad I'm a man.
7. HOLY CRAP!
8. Sure hope that sex was good.
9. I'm not really sure I'm ready for this.
10. Just be rational.

LEARNING TO COMFORT

Depending on the progress of your partner's labor, hospital protocol, and the phase of the moon (delivery nurses swear on their profession that more babies are born during a full moon), you might have to wait for a delivery room. The wait can be rather unsettling for a mother in pain, and this is a great chance to practice comforting her before things get really tough.

Comforting and soothing are activities that some guys don't do on a regular basis. But get used to it, as this is her number one emotional and physical need over the course of labor. You might even want to get in some practice before your wife goes into labor (see p. 95).

YOUR NEW HOME AWAY FROM HOME

Welcome to the room where your baby will be born: the delivery room. While your partner may be ready to give birth right away, chances are you will be here for a few hours. Some women labor in the room for twelve hours or more! (Note, however, that if the baby starts to show signs of distress or if the OB/GYN calls the game, the laboring mom will get moved on to C-section status, at which point you and your wife will be whisked to an operating room.)

After being admitted and placed in a delivery room, you are usually ensconced in your own space, where you will stay until the baby arrives. That long-term goal will be at least a few hours off, possibly considerably longer. Some hospitals sequester pre-laboring moms from moms in true labor, in which case you may

91

have to make a move to another part of the floor once the contractions start in earnest.

Here is all the gear you will find in the delivery room, and how you might interact with it. Get to know your environs and all the contraptions so you can make your and your partner's stay more comfy.

• *Adjustable bed:* Every mom has a different position that makes her comfortable during labor—sitting up, hands and knees, side, etc.—and it will change from moment to moment. Help her to move around in the bed, adjust it with the remote control, and place pillows where she wants. She may ask to be adjusted frequently, and your answer is always: "How can I help?"

• *Monitors:* Strapped to Mom's belly will be a contraction monitor hooked up to a screen and/or printer. These monitors actually show the progress of a single contraction, and you can verbally relay to your partner when a contraction seems to be receding. Anything it takes to give her some hope for relief.

• *Bathroom:* Some moms may want to use a shower for comfort. You are her shoulder to lean on when trying to make the journey across the room.

• *Pull-out couch (or at least a cushier chair):* A long labor makes for a late night. Dad might try to catch a catnap when Mom says it's okay. Just never complain about how stiff it made your back.

• *52-inch wide-screen plasma digital TV with 47 sports channels:* Don't even think about it. Even if the TV is small and not even HD, you may be tempted. But the clicker is hers. Back off.

• *Intercom to the nurses:* Although the nurses are paying really close attention to your wife through remote monitoring, the intercom is still the fastest way to let them know your wife needs something without leaving her side.

Just keep in mind that you are a man on the maternity ward. Men like to play with gadgets, and there are a lot of gadgets in this room. As Secret Agent Man, knowing and understanding these gadgets can help your wife. Plus they are interesting. But get caught snooping around too much, and you might get asked to step back.

HELP IS AT HAND:
DOULAS AND MIDWIVES

While men like gadgets, not all women are hip to the chip. Some women prefer a more organic approach to their birth and will choose to work with a midwife and/or doula.

Midwives deliver babies the old-fashioned way. Of course we will get in trouble for saying this, but we mean no harm. It's true: A midwife works with the laboring mom to deliver the baby using fewer gadgets, tubes, and probes than we have become accustomed to. This can happen out of the hospital, and sometimes even in the hospital. But don't let the low-tech vibe fool you. Midwives can handle some pretty difficult birth scenarios. At the same time, it is good to have a back-up plan if a hospital admission becomes necessary.

* One of the coolest things about midwives is that they are present. As opposed to the OB/GYN who will pop in and out, the midwife will be by Mom's side from the onset of serious contractions through the birth of the child and beyond.
* Midwives also tend to prioritize the wishes of the mother over standard hospital procedure.
* They also tend to be much more supportive of a mom's wish to have a natural childbirth.

Doulas are a throwback to a time when births were attended by all the mothers of the family, a group of supportive and experienced women. A doula is a trained and experienced woman there to provide assistance and comfort during labor, birth, and post partum. Some women really like the emotional and physical help, and of course it takes some pressure off you. As a guy you have to ask yourself if you are comfortable with another person present during this intimate time.

MAKING NICE WITH ELLEN D.

Immediately upon arrival you will meet the most important person in your delivery: the labor and delivery (L&D) nurse, whom we like to refer to as Nurse Ellen D. While the OB doesn't come in until the last minute to catch the baby, it is Ellen who will guide your wife through labor. Ellen can also set the tone for labor, and this is where you, Secret Agent Man, might step in.

* If you are lucky and Ellen is super caring and friendly to Mom, then you are set for labor. Nothing need be done. Most Ellens are this way.

* But if Ellen is a little cold, too efficient, in a bad mood, or caring for a few too many mothers, the vulnerable pregnant mom can get pretty upset. It's time for you to take control and do your best doula imitation. Compensate for the nurturing deficit. Or in more PC terms, be the partner your partner always wanted. Reset the tone without ever letting her know you are doing it.

* Regardless of Ellen D.'s demeanor, as a dad you must befriend her. Her first responsibility is to your wife and then the baby. If you want any information, it has to come through her.

* Remember that your wife is the patient. Technically you are just a bystander. You may have lots of questions or worries about Mom and the baby, but there is no "we" in patient, and you, the guest, need to tread lightly.

ELLEN D. THE SPELUNKER

Just as with your OB appointments, be prepared for Ellen to examine your pregnant partner to check how the labor is progressing. These internal exams will happen frequently, and for some dads they can be a little awkward since, unlike OB/GYN visits, your mother-in-law and your mom might be present.

After years of sneaking away from the 'rents to make out under the bleachers, suddenly your mom and her mom are sitting right there with you two on the 50-yard line. Maybe even the sister or best friends get to join the party. It's just a little weird.

Whenever Ellen shows up, it's a good idea to suggest that other family members wait outside for just a few minutes.

THE NUMBERS:
LABOR 101

Most of what goes on in the delivery room is driven by measurements of your wife's changing body, most particularly her cervix. Without getting too technical, here are some basic things that will help you understand just what is going on when a nurse snaps on the rubber gloves and starts spouting jargon.

1. The cervix begins as a thick stopper between the vagina and the uterus, assuring that the baby, placenta, and amniotic fluid all stay safely sealed in the uterus.

2. In the final weeks of pregnancy, the cervix transforms: It thins until it becomes, in medical terms, "fully effaced." Now it's ready for its next trick: dilation.

UNDILATED:

|---| ———————————————— 0 to 3 cm

PARTIALLY DILATED:

 ————————————— BABY HEAD

|-----------| ——————————— 3 to 7 cm

FULLY DILATED:

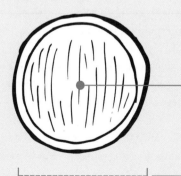 ——————————— BABY HEAD

|------------------| ——— 7 to 10 cm

3. During labor, the cervix dilates, or opens from zero to ten centimeters, in a matter of several hours. This is analogous to you opening your mouth wide enough to swallow a basketball.

The engine that drives this transformation is contractions, also known as labor, and how long that process takes varies widely from woman to woman. With a first baby, you should expect that contractions will last at least six to eight hours and will often go for ten and even longer. Labor usually gets quicker with each successive baby.

LABOR LINGO

Here are the basic stages and stations you can expect to hear batted around over the course of the final trimester office visits as well as during labor and delivery.

DILATION
• Latent or early labor: Zero to three centimeters of dilation or opening.
• Active Labor: Three to seven centimeters of dilation.
• Transitional Labor: Seven to ten centimeters

STATIONS
• 4 to -3 station: Baby is just beginning to descend into the pelvis.
• 0 station: The baby's head is engaged in the upper part of the pelvis.
• +2 to +3 station: The baby's head has passed through the pelvis.
• +5 station: The baby begins to pass through the vaginal opening, often called crowning.

If the contractions aren't progressing—i.e., getting closer and closer together and resulting in a dilation of the cervix—your doctor may elect to speed things up a bit by administering a drug called Pitocin. Pitocin is a synthetic version of the pregnancy hormone oxytocin, which causes the cervix to dilate. Giving it to a pregnant woman will quickly intensify contractions. The drug is also used to cause or "induce" labor in pregnant women who have not yet begun to have contractions. (Your OB may suggest inducing if your wife has gone beyond 40 weeks without any signs of labor beginning on its own.)

LABOR IT IS

As men, we will never know how bad labor hurts, but take it from us: We have watched both a natural childbirth (no drugs) and a medicated childbirth (drugs to ease the pain). It looks friggin' painful either way.

So what can you do?

Basically, your job in labor is to comfort the laboring mom in whatever way she wants to be comforted, be it emotional or physical, all the while knowing that her needs and desires will change. The rest of this chapter is fluff.

• Massage her until she yells at you to quit, until she cries for your help, until she never wants to be touched again, until the contraction is over and she asks you to stroke her hair.

• Play that special L&D mix you made for the iPod—the one with all of her favorites, the sweet ones, your "couple" songs, and even a few hilarious oldies. Helen Reddy, "I Am Woman," yes!

• Make her laugh, unless it hurts.

• Read to her from her favorite trashy magazine.

• Forgive her for anything she says, and always take the high road.

TAKING CARE OF DAD

Remember that you are also your own support team and soon to be the baby's support team as well. So you must take care of yourself. At the same time, since this is not about you, you will need to be stealthy and opportunistic when it comes to taking care of your needs.

1. Catnap if you can.

As we stated earlier, labor can last a long time, maybe even through the night—maybe even into more than one night. It's nature's first introduction into the hell of sleepless nights you are about to encounter. Catnap when you can—especially while the mom is able to catnap, whether from sheer exhaustion or from a temporary break in the immediate action.

2. Do not let your stomach growl during labor.

The cafeteria might be closed at night, so be prepared for the long haul with some dollar bills for the snack machines. There will be no running out for some fast food; the baby has a mind of its own and might come sooner than expected. Just remember not to eat in front of your wife, if at all possible. You just never know what might set her off at this point: food fumes or simply fuming over your apparent gustatory enjoyment.

3. Try to keep hydrated.

Another good reason to befriend the nursing staff. They can supply you with a pitcherful that you can then resupply with water as needed. Be sure to drink up. Water can do remarkable things for keeping you alert when fatigue starts to set in.

4. When possible, take a jog around the ward.

Another good way to get your circulation going and blow off a little steam when/if there's a break in the action.

5. Find your mantra. Repeat as needed.

Maybe it's as simple as telling yourself, "We're almost there," but giving yourself some positive affirmations to keep your mind focused and yourself outwardly calm for Mom's sake is a very good idea.

6. Check in with one of your boys.

Judiciously, quickly, get in a call to one of the posse, preferably one who's been through this all before, to let him know where you are in the process, and vent a little. Maybe even catch up on a score or two.

Note: Whether in search of a snack, hydration, a breath of fresh air, exercise, or a better cell phone signal, you may be tempted to step outside the hospital for just a moment. Always a dicey move, especially at night. Just ask Daddy Brad. He bolted to fetch the camera from the car and found himself locked out of the building as the birth of his daughter rapidly approached. Avoid looking like an escaped mental patient, flailing your arms in the night, by staying put and not leaving the building after hours.

LABOR TIME WARP

One question comes up again and again throughout labor: How much longer? The answer is: Nobody knows. In addition, there's this weird time warp that happens in delivery rooms, especially when the proceedings take place late at night. Time drags and races and warps with an almost hallucinogenic trippiness. Get ready:

- Labor is divided roughly between contractions and pushing.
- The contractions phase is subdivided into pre-labor, active labor, and transitional labor, each defined by the number of centimeters the cervix is dilated. How long any of these phases will last is anybody's guess and varies wildly from woman to woman and even from pregnancy to pregnancy. This may explain women's endless ability to throw these stats around like fantasy baseball geeks at draft time.
- Usually, the contractions take longer than the pushing, but beyond that, the phases of labor may be measured in minutes, hours, or days.
- Pre-labor—when the cervix is dilated more or less 1 to 4 centimeters—is cruelly named. Your wife will be in acute pain, perhaps vocalizing through the contraction, really letting you know about it, when the nurse or doctor performs a quick internal check and informs you that she is still in pre-labor. The appropriate response in this situation is: "You've got to be shitting me. PRE-labor?!" It's at this point that the rubber hits the road in terms of pain management.

PAIN MANAGEMENT:
THE ETERNAL EPIDURAL QUESTION

During labor, your wife will be given some options for pain relief. Beyond nonmedical methods such as massage, drugs can be a mom's friend. It is very important that you talk through the options with your doctor beforehand, because once your wife is in pain, you might become part of her decision-making process. She will look to you to help her decide. And why would one have to decide? Isn't it a no-brainer? Not exactly.

Avoiding pain and suffering is good, but anesthesia carries some risk of dangerous side effects, may slow the delivery, and is shared by Mom and baby alike. With drugs on board, the baby may struggle to breastfeed immediately after birth. Considering all this, some women will elect "natural" or drug-free childbirth.

For moms electing to say a resounding "yes" to drugs, however, the options begin in the pre-labor phase, when an intravenous "cocktail" may be administered. Some moms like fighting the pain aggressively, others find the associated grogginess to be unpleasant.

The most common form of labor pain relief is the epidural. This procedure basically involves a giant needle being stuck into her back in a manner that looks a lot like a scene from *The Matrix*, only lower down on the spine. The timing of the epidural is critical, as it must happen in a limited window: The epidural can only be performed after active labor has locked in (as it can slow or disrupt the progression of labor), but before transitional labor, when Mom is preparing to push. (Note: It's a good idea to have Mom's cervix checked a final time immediately before the epidural is inserted, particularly if she has gotten up or moved around since the last check. Things can progress and change quickly.)

1. Be prepared for the fear factor.
From out of nowhere, an anesthesiologist will waltz in, and nonchalantly he (yes he, one of the few men you might hang with during labor) or she will explain all the dangers of what is about to happen, should your wife choose to accept it. While things rarely go wrong, the danger is real, and this may be the first time the whole thing gets medically scary for you. (Your wife, on the other hand, will likely already be far beyond the point of scaring.)

2. *Realize that you may not have much time to debate the issue.*
Not only does it look scary, but there are real dangers. You are dealing with the spine here, and everything from paralysis to death is possible, though statistically unlikely.

3. *Do your homework.*
Reading about the dangers beforehand might help you to be better informed, or it might really scare you into considering the natural route. She'll probably still want the drugs.

4. *Don't faint.*
This happens more than you would expect. Anesthesiologists tell stories of dads hitting the deck and becoming patients themselves. Be strong for your wife, but don't force yourself to be a man and watch something that will cause you to go vasovagal.

(By the way, anesthesiologists get paid on average $325,000 their first year out of med school. Don't complain; after all, he or she needs to have the skill to make spinal injections. At the same time you can bet he or she is not driving a minivan. But we digress into stereotypes.)

ABOUT THIS WHOLE NATURAL CHILDBIRTH THING . . .

Regardless of how committed Mom is to having a natural childbirth, there will come a point at which she gives strong reconsideration to this decision. If a midwife or doula is present, she will be very helpful in helping Mom through this moment of doubt. A traditional L&D nurse is much more likely to strongly encourage an epidural, leaving you holding the birth plan. It's a tough spot. One you should game a bit before labor begins.

• Suggesting that Mom take just one more minute, one more contraction, one more hour before making the decision may help her avoid regrets later.

• If she insists, take the high road: Listen to her, tell her it won't change a thing in your mind—she's still your hero, meds or no meds. And be thankful that it's not you.

CROWNING:
THE GREATEST EUPHEMISM OF ALL TIME

Labor progresses. Pre-labor becomes active labor becomes transitional labor. The contractions widen the opening of the cervix and force the baby down the birth canal, becoming more forceful and more closely spaced along the way. Mom is becoming more and more focused, less aware or concerned with her surroundings. At some point in the later stages of the contractions, a nurse announces that the baby is "crowning."

This sounds so regal, so elegant, so suggestive of achievement that you can't help having a look. What you see is a purplish, slimy, hairy eggplant, well past its prime, emerging from what was once the "magic place." Never in your life has one piece of landscape been so radically transformed.

Which begs the question: Should you look? Crowning is just the "Coming Attractions." The action/adventure movie is still to come. Dads have become the key attendant for most moms, but does that obligate a guy to bear witness to every emission and emergence?

In our opinion, a neck-up approach is completely legit, as long as that approach is communicated ahead of time. But be warned: Even the least squeamish dad has to be ready, because the sounds and smells of delivery are as strong as the sights. Bathroom smells mingle with medical smells and the metallic smell of blood. You may hear or even feel your wife tear. To avoid all of these experiences, you'd have to leave the room, and take a big step back a generation or two.

If you do elect to watch, you will see a miracle, but you may never look at your partner's body the same way. For many this is a transition, like becoming a parent. A transformative experience that is a rich moment in life. She changes. You change.

PUSH!

At some point during transitional labor, Mom will start to get the urge to push.

1. Depending on the progress of the labor, Mom may be encouraged to go with or to resist this urge.

2. It's usually at this point that the OB is called in and takes the lead in the delivery room.

3. The level of activity picks up considerably, with nurses helping Mom into the stirrups, draping her, firing up the warming table, and generally preparing for the arrival of the baby.

4. This is a good time for you to plant yourself at Mom's side for the foreseeable. Try not to move around too much, as the pros are really swinging into action now.

5. The pushing, unlike the contractions, is a voluntary action, pretty much like going to the bathroom, but let's not linger on the analogy. The doctor/nurses will coach, usually encouraging Mom

to work with the contractions and to sustain her efforts in order to keep the baby moving.

The emergence of the head is a mind-blowing moment of life coming into existence beyond our power of description. It takes a bit more work to clear a shoulder, and then the baby is born in a rush of fluids. And she is suddenly and fully here. Pinkish blue, smeared with whitish grease, prizefighter-faced and tiny. But here.

There are many before and after moments in your life. The day you learned to ride a bike. Your first kiss. Graduation. Your first real job. Getting married. All of these are nothing compared to having a kid. The following may grate on the ears of your non-breeder friends, but it's true nonetheless: Having a child changes you in ways they will never understand. And a key moment in this is the actual birth. Far be it from us to tell you how you are going to feel. So we won't. Suffice to say that you will have some thoughts and feelings that you never knew were inside you.

BY THE BOOK VS. REALITY

In a textbook birth, labor and delivery are predictable and manageable; everything they told you about in birthing class happens exactly as you were taught. But reality has a nasty way of asserting itself just when you least want it to.

To recap, in a textbook birth:

- Ellen D. goes spelunking.
- She notes that the cervix is sufficiently dilated, and that it is time for Mom to push.

- She alerts the OB/GYN.
- Your OB/GYN rushes over.
- The OB/GYN is actually your own OB/GYN—the one you planned on being there on the big day.
- Mom grabs Dad's hand and squeezes tightly.
- Mom pushes a few times.
- Baby is delivered.

And so it happens on TV and in the movies. But in real life, not so much. In real life, there are far too many ways things can go differently. But here's a partial list, just for starters:

- The cervix stalls and never reaches 10 cm. Pitocin is used to induce.
- Another doctor is on call; yours is skiing in Aspen.
- Mom has to push for a long, long time, and it's really painful.
- The perineum (the tissue between vagina and anus) tears or is cut (called an episiotomy) during delivery and must be stitched back up.
- The baby is in distress, and Mom is rushed off for an unplanned C-section (see p. 110).
- The baby has difficulty making it out of the womb. Ellen D. or your doctor reposition the baby, the baby has a hard time exiting, or Mom is rushed off for a C-section.
- The baby comes before the doctor arrives.
- Dad passes out when he elects to watch the C-section.

Regardless of the course of events, a baby is born. But there is still plenty of birthing business to do.

CUTTING THE CORD:
FORGING NEW BONDS

Are you a cord cutter? If you are, the OB will offer you a chance to ply your trade immediately after the birth of your child. The doc will place clamps on either side of where the cut should be made on the umbilical cord, and offer you a pair of medical scissors. Be warned: This thing is called a cord for a reason. It has the look, feel, and thickness of a healthy length of rope. It offers plenty of resistance. Not for the squeamish.

Even as all this cord chopping is going on, your baby is taking his first quiz, called an APGAR test. This is a quick and simple way, based largely on the appearance of the baby, that his or her health is evaluated by the doc (see page 116). If the score is a 7 or higher, the baby will get a quick aspiration of the nostrils and mouth with a little rubber thingy, a gush of some gunky eyedrops to guard against infection, and then be returned to Mom's chest or tummy. If everything has gone smoothly, Mom and new baby will be given some time to bond and perhaps even try nursing for the first time. A sweet moment. Maybe the sweetest ever.

After a few moments, the nurse may take the baby back to measure his specs, wrap him snug in a swaddling blanket, and put him in his first skully.

AFTER BIRTH

Meanwhile, back at the uterus, work continues.

1. Even though the baby has been born, Mom will continue to have intense physical, and maybe even psychological, side effects for hours, and even days, to come.

2. In the hour or so immediately after the delivery, Mom will continue to have smaller contractions until she delivers the placenta, which is the organ that served as the fetus's life support system in the uterus. It looks like bumpy liver. (It's a little sad that this amazing, life-giving organ produced by Mom along with the baby will now simply be dumped in with the medical waste, but that doesn't make us any more inclined to save it or, ew, eat it.)

3. Even after the placenta is delivered, Mom will continue to be treated to hours of intense cramps, which serve to contract the uterus. These cramps may get more painful as the anesthesia wears off. The cramps force all the remaining fluids, blood, and matter out of the uterus. And there is a lot. So much so that you'll probably see a lot of the big, flat diaper-like mini-blankets that the nurses frequently replace under Mom. Eventually she'll graduate to a handsome pair of jumbo-sized mesh panties that you won't be seeing in a swimsuit calendar anytime soon, but they certainly serve a purpose: to hold mega-maxi pads in place (see page 127). She will need this rig for two or three days and continue to experience lighter and lighter discharge over the next ten days or so.

4. An hour or two passes, and Dad now has a big decision to make here, along with Mom. The baby is about to be taken to a

nursery to be more thoroughly cleaned and examined. You can either go with the kid or stay with Mom. Going with the kid allows Mom a chance to compose herself and allays those fears that someone is going to mix up or steal your baby. (Don't worry about this too much; hospitals tag your baby almost immediately as he or she exits the womb.) If you stay with Mom, you'll have the chance to collect yourselves as new parents. It's a great time to reflect on the mountain you, she, and baby have just climbed. (More on this in the next chapter.)

A SPECIAL SECTION ABOUT C-SECTIONS

Planned or not, a C-section is major surgery and nothing to sneeze at. In order to deliver the baby, the surgeon will be cutting through abdominal muscles and moving major vital organs around. Weirdly enough, many hospitals allow you to be present to observe the whole procedure!

1. When it is time for your wife's C-section, she will be transferred to a gurney and wheeled to the Obstetrical Operating Room.
2. While she is being prepped for surgery, you will don scrubs and wait in a prescribed area.
3. While you are waiting, Mom will be given both a spinal anesthetic and perhaps another medication to ease her discomfort.
4. When you enter, you'll see Mom only from about the collarbone up; the rest will be hidden behind a curtain of sterile drapes.
5. The OB/GYN, an anesthesiologist, nurses, and perhaps a perinatologist will be present.
6. You will sit next to Mom's head and comfort her through the operation. She may shiver as a result of the anesthesia, but this is completely normal.

7. The baby will be delivered through an incision made below the belly button through the abdominal muscles and the wall of the uterus.

8. Mom may be asked to push to help the doctor to deliver the baby.

9. Once the baby is delivered, you'll get a chance to say hello before she's taken to the nursery.

10. The OB will suture Mom's uterus and stomach, and Mom will return to a recovery room.

Though C-section delivery has its own risks and rewards, the result is usually the same as a vaginal birth—a beautiful baby. (In fact, Caesarian babies tend to be prettier because they haven't had to make the tough trip through the birth canal.)

Recovery from a C-section, however, is different from that of a vaginal birth. While the birth canal has been spared trauma, the incision cuts abdominal muscles and creates bleeding in the uterus. This blood may continue to issue for several days. Mom and baby will likely stay in the hospital a few days longer. The surgery, while routine, is really hard on a woman's body. She is going to need a lot of help over the next few days, especially once you get home, since she'll have some restrictions on climbing stairs, driving, and other physical tasks.

CHAPTER 7

LIFE AFTER BIRTH

THE FIRST 48 HOURS

And breathe . . .

Mom has just endured the most physical and emotional journey of her life, and while not so much physical for you, the past 8 to 28 hours (yes, labor can last that long, and longer) have been one of the wildest rides of your life.

You are now the father of another human being. And not just any old human being, but an honest-to-goodness version of you—kind of like You 2.0. If you are the type of guy who becomes really jazzed when you get a new dog or high-definition television, this is the big time. We are talking HUGE!

So what the hell do you do now?

First lesson of DadHood, and never forget this . . .

HOLD THAT BABY!

Don't be afraid to hold that baby. In the first few moments after the delivery of your child, make sure you look into that little face and realize what has just happened. Don't worry 'bout getting your shirt dirty: Newborn infants are quite disgusting, covered in white stuff (vernix) and all sorts of other goo, so be prepared. You can go to the dry cleaners later.

But cherish this moment. We're not touchy-feely guys, but believe us: You need to hold that baby. As a matter of fact, keep holding that baby as he grows. Hold him often. Hold him until he's so big he squirms out of your arms and says, "Awwwwwww, Dad, let me down!"

OK, enough of the mushy part.

TICK TOCK:
A MAN WITH A PLAN

You are now on the clock and it is ticking.

You are now responsible for the life of another human being, and so it is time to start thinking and acting like a provider. This means planning and management right out of the gate.

First order of business is to make sure you know exactly how much time Mom and baby may stay in the hospital. Ask the labor and delivery nurses how much time you have until checkout because there are numerous tasks you must accomplish during this period.

On your mark, get set, go!

KNOW THE SCORES

As you learned in the last chapter, immediately after you and Mom have a chance to meet and hold your new addition, the labor and delivery nurses will take him or her to the warming table, which is typically located in the delivery room right next to the bed. The nurses will:

- Do a quick cleanup
- Take the first round of vital statistics known as the APGAR score
- Throw on the first diaper
- Take baby footprints
- Swaddle the little munchkin

It's important to pay attention during this process because there are a few statistics you will need to remember.

1. The APGAR score.

The APGAR helps doctors and nurses assess the general health of your baby at birth by monitoring Appearance, Pulse, Grimace, Activity, and Respiration. The test is given at one minute after birth and repeated five minutes after birth. A "perfect" score is a cumulative 10, with each category scored between 0 and 2. Scores of 7 and above are normal. Get familiar with the scoring system and how it relates to your child's initial health. (Be sure to ask your OB/GYN for a quick advance lesson at one of the third trimester visits you attend.)

2. The stuff everyone will want to know.

The second set of stats are the ones you must commit to memory so you can alert the world to the birth. If you miss any of these numbers, you will be the brunt of jokes from all of your female friends and family for the rest of your days. Don't let this happen to you.

You must absolutely know the sex, weight, length, time of birth, name, and physical status of both Mom and baby (as in, "Mom and baby are doing great!"). Commit these to memory, and you're golden.

SAY TEES!

• Bring several plain white T-shirts along in your travel bag, and get them out when the nurses start assessing the infant on the warming table.

• When they take the footprints for the baby's birth record identification certificate, ask if you can also get your child's little baby footprints on the T-shirts.

• These make great gifts for the grandparents, but can also be used as props to embarrass the child when she becomes a teenager.

MAKE THE CALLS

And now it's time to share the good news with the outside world. While every new dad's call list will be different, most begin with calls to the proud grandparents, if they are not already in the lobby waiting for the news. Next up: siblings and special friends and family. Steal a page from the wedding handbook and appoint a "best man" to spread the word:

1. Hook up your best man with an e-mail and call list several weeks prior to the due date.

2. After you call the grandparents and the top spots on your list, call him with the specs and let him send out the e-mail blast and work the phone tree.

3. This ensures that everyone gets the word quickly, and you don't have to decide in which order to alert friends. You can spend that time saved with your new child!

NICE WORK, HON. NOW HERE'S A LITTLE SOMETHING FOR YOUR PAIN AND SUFFERING

As soon as the specs are complete, you and Mom will have a few more minutes of snuggle time with the new arrival. Mom may even attempt to breastfeed for the first time—babies can work up quite an appetite on the long journey through the birth canal. After your initial bonding session, the nurses will take the baby to the nursery to do some more extensive testing and blood work. At this point you may stay with Mom or tag along with your baby. This is an individual decision based on personal wishes. Some Moms may want to have a few moments to collect themselves— and, more important, she may want you to keep the baby in sight.

117

Others may want you to stay in the room right by their side. Let Mom make the call.

Regardless of whether you stay or go, find a quick private moment to let Mom know what a miraculous thing she has just accomplished. This can also be a good time to present the new mom with a birth gift that commemorates one of the most joyous occasions in your lives. Some guys pop the present while Mom is still giddy with emotion from labor and delivery; others will choose to wait until she is transferred into a recovery room before presenting the goods. The point is: Be careful here. We are talking about something that is sentimental and expresses your love, such as jewelry or a very special "I Love You" item. Stay away from things like blenders and lingerie.

After thirty minutes or so, the nurses will bring your child back into the delivery room, and you can commence staring at this incredible new creature.

A LITTLE R&R

Depending on your hospital, anywhere from four to eight hours after delivery of the baby, Mom will most likely be transferred from the birthing room to a recovery room. This is your standard hospital room without all the fancy baby delivery gear. Usually these rooms are on halls with other new parents, but not always, so be mindful of other folks who may not be visiting the hospital for the same joyous reason you are. After Mom is settled into her new home for the next few days, your focus should be devoted to accomplishing the following tasks:

- Getting Mom and baby some rest.
- Establishing a successful cycle of breastfeeding.

THE VELVET ROPE

Managing visitors is one of Dad's most important jobs in the hours after delivery, but it's not without its complications. Traffic in the delivery and recovery rooms can reach rush-hour levels.

Even if you don't have friends and family crowding in to see the new baby, there will still be a fair amount of traffic from the pros. In the first twenty-four hours of life, your child will get a visit from

- the hospital pediatrician
- the baby photographer who holds the concession with the hospital
- a hospital staffer with paperwork for the birth certificate
- a tech to give a hearing test
- a tech to test for jaundice
- the lactation consultant
- the Labor and Delivery nurses
- the OB/GYN

119

Then of course there's the steady stream of family and well-wishers who are chomping at the bit to come see the baby. First decide whether you and your wife want visitors or instead prefer a bit more privacy. If you accept visitors, by all means don't let folks just drop by. Decide exactly who gets an entry ticket, and give them very specific times to visit. Keep an eye on Mom and the baby, and don't be afraid to play traffic cop when either or both need a rest. Work the velvet rope if you have to. Mom will appreciate it—and visitors will generally be understanding.

With traffic flow managed to a tolerable level, it's time to get Mom some rest. For the majority of your stay in the hospital, the baby will be in the room with you, peacefully snoozing in the bassinet next to Mom's bed. However, at times newborns can be a little fussy, so remember that the nurses will, at any time of the day or night, take your baby back to the nursery and take great care of the little one. Don't be afraid to take advantage of this!

LATCH ON, BABY

The second order of business is to establish a consistent breast-feeding routine. Hopefully your little one started feeding right out of the chute, and by the time he gets back from the first round of diagnostic testing, he will be ready for another helping of flapjacks, so to speak. If all goes well, the cycle will work like this:

1. About every two hours, around the clock, you'll start by changing the baby. This will get him or her nice and fussy and awake—and that's a good thing. Sleepy newborns don't feed well.

2. Then Mom will take over, initially feeding the baby for about five to ten minutes on each breast. She'll take a break to burp the wee one before moving him to the other breast. You will be given the opportunity to burp the little one after mealtime, so do your part, burp master.

3. By the end of the feeding, the baby will, hopefully, be groggy and ready to go back to sleep.

4. Rinse and repeat.

Now, it won't always work as simply as that. There will be times when the baby is fussy or won't wake up as scheduled. None of this ever goes perfectly.

- If Mom starts to feel physical discomfort—sore nipples, difficulty getting into a comfortable position—or seems anxious or frustrated with the process, keep encouraging her. Some babies just can't properly latch on at first.

- Remember, there are professionals available to offer assistance: The Labor and Delivery nurses can offer tips and advice while Mom and baby are still in the hospital.

- Don't be afraid to call in the big guns—a.k.a. the lactation consultant. A lactation consultant is someone whose sole job is to assist new mothers in figuring out how to breastfeed. Most hospitals have one on staff who will assist during your stay, and you can also hire a consultant after you go home from the hospital. It may sound strange to hire a consultant for such a natural process as breastfeeding, but believe us, if Mom and baby are having difficulties, a good lactation consultant is worth her weight in colostrum.

BABY BUFFET; OR, LATIN FOR NEWBORNS

So what the hell is *colostrum*?

Glad you asked. It's essentially super food for babies. During late pregnancy and immediately following birth, female mammals produce this substance, also known as "first milk," as a ready snack for the newborn. High in carbohydrates, protein, and antibodies, but very low in fat, this stuff is packed with nutrients.

And not only that—it also acts as poop lube. That's right, it performs as a mild laxative to encourage baby's first poop, which also has a funny name: *meconium*. Meconium is a black, sticky, tarlike substance that constitutes your child's first growler and contains material the infant ingested in the uterus. Resembling a congealed chunk of Vaseline-covered mole sauce, meconium is not pretty, but here's the kicker: It is *odorless*. No stink, nada, zilch. This presents you with a perfect opportunity to change your child's first diaper in a stink-free environment.

FIG. A

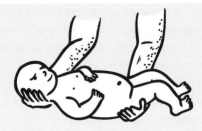

FIG. B

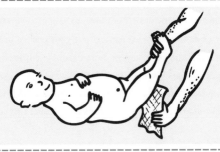

FIG. C

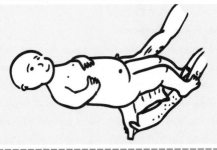

FIG. D

Do it, man. Don't be scared. Ask the Labor and Delivery nurse to walk you through the process. It is much easier to learn the intricacies of diaper changing with a cute little meconium load instead of waiting for a heaping, steaming diaper full of hotdogs and grape skins. Trust us. This is the preseason, so practice your skills now while there are skilled coaches around; you are going to need them once the regular season starts.

HOW TO PROPERLY CHANGE A NEWBORN'S DIAPER

1. Place baby faceup on the changing table, making sure to constantly support the back of the head and neck. (Fig. A)
2. Make a joke about how tiny the infant is by using cornball analogies like "knee-high to a grasshopper" and "smaller than a gnat's balls."
3. Remove diaper and check to see if wet and/or soiled.
4. Record findings in log book (see page 125).
5. If wet only, proceed to step 7.
6. If soiled, make intelligent yet smart-ass comment about the texture and sliminess of meconium.
7. Carefully wipe baby's diaper area clean with wet wipes. (Fig. B)
8. Place infant's bottom on clean diaper by gently lifting legs and sliding Velcro end under bum. (Fig. C)
9. Fold top of diaper over and affix with Velcro tabs. (Fig. D)
10. Swaddle baby in blanket.
11. Hand baby to Mom for a huge meal.
12. Celebrate inwardly while maintaining an "it was nothing" demeanor on the outside.

123

One final important note about breastfeeding: For some new moms and babies, despite repeated efforts and lots of frustration, breastfeeding just won't take. For these folks, formula is a lifesaver, literally. Mom may be deeply disappointed and have feelings of failure associated with giving the baby formula. Remind her that formula is a miracle of modern science and that a healthy baby is the main objective. Tell her it's nice for you because now you can feed the baby, too. Lovingly prepared and served by either parent, formula provides plenty of nutrition and comfort to your hungry little one.

CAPTAIN'S LOG, STAR DATE:
NEWBORN

A healthy newborn usually pinches a meconium nugget within the first 12 hours of life and gets its whiz on within 24 hours. This input and output information needs to be recorded in a logbook. The doctors and nurses will monitor this information closely, so it's important to keep careful track. Take over the paperwork so your wife can concentrate on bonding with the baby and resting. It cannot be said too many times that rest helps the recovery process and fatigue makes for emotional and physical discomfort.

DATE	TIME FEEDING BEGINS	TIME FEEDING ENDS	WET DIAPER	POOP	POOP NOTES

TAKING CARE OF OTHER BUSINESS

After the commotion has settled and Mom is working on some shut-eye, it's time to regroup and tie up any loose ends. If there are things to tend to, this is your chance.

• Do you need sleep? Take advantage of this respite, and head back to your house to grab a wink. If this is not possible, take a nap on the pullout in the hospital room.

• Is the fridge stocked for homecoming at your abode? If not, now is your chance to run to the grocery and grab some grub. Remember, healthy fare is best: Nursing women can be voracious eaters.

• Do you have pets at home that need to be fed or mail to be gathered? Take care of these while Mom is napping.

• Just remember: This is not a license to be AWOL for long periods. Take care of your business and get back to the hospital. Your family needs a man around.

PREPARE FOR TAKEOFF

Some vital information before you, Mom, and baby prepare for departure:

1.   According to most hospital regulations, Mom must be able to poop and pee before she heads for home; this is a surefire sign that she is on her way to recovery.

2. She will still likely be experiencing tremendous discomfort in the nether regions, especially if there was tearing of the perineum during the delivery. There are numerous treatments for this discomfort that we, as men, have no ability to comprehend; the important thing is to pamper Mom as much as possible.

3. She will also be experiencing lochia: a normal vaginal discharge that occurs after birth. Due to the lochia, she will wear big-ass mesh grandma panties. We're not kidding: These things look like the cheesecloth diapers Godzilla wears after he gets old and becomes incontinent. We're telling you this not so that you can think up some clever jokes to crack, but so that you will be prepared not to laugh. Hold your tongue, dude, hold your tongue.

HUNTING AND SCAVENGING

So, your forty-eight hours are running out. Mom is up and about a little, though still pretty sore and fragile. The sleeping and feeding cycle is established, and it's time to start wrapping up.

First of all, take everything that isn't tied down, because you paid for it. The hospital bassinet is a treasure trove packed with diapers, blankets, wipes, creams, snot suckers, and jams and jellies of all types. Pick it clean.

Mom will probably also have some prescriptions to fill. Go ahead and take care of those before you leave the hospital—maybe while Mom and baby are having a nap. If they don't have a pharmacy, or if it is after hours, go to a local drugstore and fill the prescriptions. Do not wait to fill the prescription on the way home!

BUCKLE UP

The final vitally important step once the doctors have discharged Mom and baby is to put your child in the car-seat carrier. Studies suggest that more than half of car seats are installed improperly. Do your homework and make sure you can install your baby carrier according to manufacturer specifications. But do not wait until you are ready to check out to begin this process.

1.   Practice with a car seat and a doll—though if you're really trying to approximate reality, you might use a sack of golf balls or an octopus. Newborns have little muscle tone and like to be tightly swaddled.

2.   We recommend that you use an insert that fits inside the seat and supports the baby's head. Since the newborn lacks the muscle

FIG. A

Models vary, but most car seats are installed with a lap or shoulder strap.

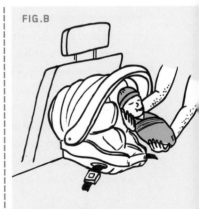

FIG.B

Gently supporting the head and neck, place the baby in the car seat.

strength to keep his head steady, he'll need a little extra support the first few weeks.

3. Make sure the straps are snug, but with enough slack for you to fit a finger underneath. The center buckle should be three to four inches beneath the chin.

4. You won't be able to keep your floppy newborn from shifting once you're in motion, so do the best you can, and drive carefully.

The nurses will make you demonstrate that you can correctly secure the infant before they let you leave. But with this task accomplished, you are on your own.

In fact, there's only one more directive to concern yourself with at this point: Begin family life!

129

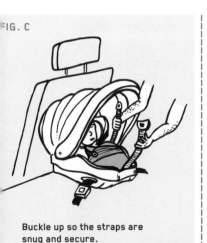

FIG. C

Buckle up so the straps are snug and secure.

FIG. D

The center buckle should be 3 to 4 inches below the chin.

DAD RANT

DADDY BRAD

Having watched *Lady and the Tramp*, I was concerned that bringing a new baby into the family was going to be a big adjustment for my faithful canine companion Percy, a 185-pound mastiff Rottweiler mix. So I planned to introduce Percy to my newborn son's smell by bringing home some blankets in which the baby had been swaddled.

Unfortunately, when I packed the blankets I also added a carton of beef fajitas left over from our delivery-room postbirth celebration feast. By the time the blankets reached Percy's nose, they smelled more like skirt steak than new baby.

Now I know that you should never leave an infant alone with a dog, no matter how docile, trusted, friendly, young, old, cute, and toothless the dog may be. I was diligent about this with our son, and thank goodness. Because, to this day, although Percy has come to love and protect the newest member of our family, every time he lays eyes on our son, he looks like I do when I'm about to enjoy a big plate of nachos.

CHAPTER 8

POSTPARTUM

SEX, SOME OTHER STUFF, AND SEX

Ever crap out a watermelon? Not a little cantaloupe: a big Fourth of July watermelon. Try it sometime. And before you do it, grow the watermelon inside your colon for the better part of a year. After you've successfully passed the watermelon, you will have begun to get a small idea of what birth is like.

Whether a natural birth or one with every painkiller in the book, it's a wild body and mind experience that your partner just went through. But hey, now the baby is born. You get your wife back! Everything is back to normal. Stitch her up, and I'll take her home!

Not quite.

Those first weeks and months after the birth are filled with all kinds of challenges for your partner, your newborn, and you. In the next chapter we will dig into your baby's world a little. But for now, let's take a look at the woman who just accomplished the watermelon trick.

NEWBORN

WATERMELON

THE MIRACLE OF LIFE HURTS LIKE HELL!

Ever played a game of backyard football and woke up the next day stiff and sore? Try squeezing that football out of your urethra. Your partner is going to be feeling it. Add hormones and early breastfeeding, and you've got one worked-out woman.

In those early weeks your partner might be dealing with pulled muscles, aching joints and back, numbness, tingling, incontinence, pains in the goodies, and a few other fun surprises. Your job is to help. Be a hero for a while. If you can, clear some time to help around the house during recovery or get some help from neighbors and family.

Some couples opt for a postpartum doula. A birth doula assists during labor. A postpartum doula helps guide a couple in those first weeks home. Some will help clean or prepare a meal, even give some diapering lessons. Many postpartum doulas are also trained massage therapists. This can be a true godsend for a new mother.

DID I HEAR SOMETHING TEAR?

The perineum is the area between the urethra and the anus, otherwise known as that space between the pee-pee hole and poop-chute. It can also be called the taint or the chode, but usually not by medical experts. It has a helluva time in birth. It's designed to stretch out and occasionally rips to help the baby pass into the world. Sometimes an obstetrician or midwife may choose to cut the perineum before it rips. This is called an episiotomy. An episiotomy is easier to sew up, but recent studies show that a natural tear tends to heal more easily. Either one takes some home care.

133

1. Keeping the perineum clean with showers and baths will help, as will keeping Mom well hydrated. This makes for easier bowel movements and less strain on the healing perineum. Remember when your trash bag ripped before you got it down to the end of the drive? You don't want a repeat of that!

2. Sitz baths are great, too. A sitz bath is like a hot tub for the naughties. Mom sits and soaks up to her hips for about twenty minutes in warm water. A good soak can ease a lot of the postbirth discomfort. You can also add Epsom salt or herbs to help the healing. You can find these at most pharmacies.

3. Popping a couple of ibuprofen tablets will also help with the pain and swelling. Of course, when breastfeeding it's always a good idea to remember that whatever mother ingests, baby ingests. But according to the American Academy of Pediatrics, ibuprofen is perfectly safe for a breastfeeding mother.

4. You can also invest in a donut cushion. Not the coolest accessory to have, but it sure eases chode pain while Mom is sitting.

SHOULDN'T I BE HAPPY RIGHT NOW?

- Your partner is crying and doesn't know why.
- She's exhausted, but can't seem to sleep.
- She's pulled out her Morrissey CDs and is playing them on repeat.
- The baby is healthy, the day is sunny, but she feels blue.

This is normal. But it's not fun.

THE EMOTIONAL STUFF: BABY BLUES

Most new mothers experience a period of mood swings, sadness, and/or lack of energy in the first week or so after the birth. This is commonly called the "baby blues."

After birth, a woman's hormones that have aided the pregnancy and birth tank out, and a new batch of breastfeeding hormones get to work. This is perfectly natural, but it can feel lousy. Mix that with exhaustion and the emotional strangeness of suddenly being a parent, and you get a mom who might not be feeling herself.

It's particularly difficult dealing with the baby blues when everyone is expecting her to be the smiling new mother. Dad, make sure you don't join the chorus. "Hey babe, you should be thrilled! Come on, buck up!" That doesn't help. Your job is to help her through.

• Give her a break so she can take a walk or talk with a friend.

• Order her favorite take-out food and rent a silly movie for the two of you to watch.

• Provide rest, food, and support from family and friends; they can be key to riding out these early days.

But sometimes the feelings are a little severe. Read on.

POSTPARTUM DEPRESSION

About 1 in 10 new mothers experiences postpartum depression sometime in their first year of motherhood. And it kind of sucks. She might have unexpected weight loss or gain, sleeping problems, crying spells, a desire to avoid the baby, and perhaps an overall feeling that life is a big pile of poo.

Postpartum depression is a medical condition and can be a serious challenge for both you and the new mom. It can be difficult for a man to see his partner crying for no apparent reason. We want to be the logical-fix-it-guy. "Tell me the problem, and I'll solve it." But depression doesn't work that way. This is your chance to be the super-supportive sensitive guy and not try to convince her she shouldn't be feeling like crap.

1. Let your partner feel what she's feeling. She's not going crazy; she's going through a very common postbirth stage.

2. Give her some space. Help with the chores and call on your support community of friends and family to help. Get Grandma to watch the baby for an hour and go for a drive together.

3. Encourage her to take some breaks, even short ones, to go for a walk, read a book, see a movie, or get together with friends. She might not be at a place where she can reach out to others. Go ahead and call her closest friends and ask them to drop by.

4. You might also want to consult your doctor, especially if symptoms grow more serious. Postpartum depression can lead to feelings of shame or guilt, even thoughts of suicide or harming the baby. Your doctor can recommend a counselor or therapist and, in some cases, antidepressants. How this will affect breastfeeding is something for you, your partner, and your doctor to discuss.

POSTPARTUM ANXIETY AND PSYCHOSIS

In certain cases a new mom can drift into some rougher waters. Postpartum anxiety includes symptoms of insomnia, extreme anxiety, and thoughts or urges to hurt the baby.

In the rare occasion (1 in a 1,000) a woman can suffer from postpartum psychosis with hallucinations, delusions, and frantic energy. In both these cases, contact a doctor immediately—but you probably already guessed that.

Hey, you're freaking my shit out!

Okay, this chapter has some scary stuff. Don't freak out. You're going to be fine. We just want you to have a heads-up for some of the challenges heading your way. If you want to learn more about these issues, check out www.postpartum.net or www.depressionafterdelivery.com. You might also read Marrit Ingman's hilarious and honest memoir of postpartum depression, *Inconsolable: How I Threw My Mental Health Out with the Diapers.* It's a great book and includes the term *buttplug.* You'll have to read it to find out why.

137

SUPPORT:
WON'T YOU BE MY NEIGHBOR?

Maybe you were taught that a real man needs no one's assistance. A true stud stands alone. Maybe you're the Rambo of fathering, sprinting through the jungles of paternity with a diaper and a machine gun. Well, get over it and ask for help.

New parents need a community: friends who drop a meal by during those first few weeks, family members who watch the baby for a bit, and other young parents with whom they can commiserate about the struggles and wonders of this new life in your home.

1. Don't be afraid to ask for a favor or two. Grandparents are freaking drooling over the chance to be left alone with the baby, and friends with older kids are happy to help. They remember. Even your childless friends (some of them, at least) will get a huge kick out being a part of the adventure. Plus, you'll offer a hand when it's their turn.

2. Online parenting communities can also be an excellent source of friends and insight. Find one that works for you. Often these groups organize meals or chore help for members in the first few weeks with a newborn.

3. Let your needs be known. Again, it might seem counter to your manly ideal, but swallow that pride and help your community help you. Call the grandparents, send out the e-mail blast to friends, and generally get the word passed that you are ready, willing, and able to receive help.

HOLY CRAP. YOU, TOO?

Find some father friends. Meet them for a beer or a cigar or a plate of buffalo wings. A few fellow fathers you can swap poop and snot stories with are priceless. Encourage your partner to do the same. Send her off for a Mama's Night Out and make sure you get a few Dad's Nights Out. The house will be a happier place for it.

Invite friends over, let their kids play in your yard, let them hold your baby, and tell them to bring beer or you won't let them in the door. It's great to know that you're not alone in this weird wonderful ride we call parenting.

SEX:
CAN WE NOW?

Most likely you won't be getting lucky that first week or so. The region needs a rest, especially if there's been an episiotomy or tearing. At one point experts felt a woman should wait six weeks before engaging in a healthy bout of naughty knocking. But now doctors say that if there's no bleeding or fever, you two can go at it whenever you feel ready.

That means when you *both* feel ready, so cool your jets.

Some couples return to sex after two weeks. Others take a few months. And you might find your partner wants to hold off on penetration for some time. If that's the case, be creative:

* Make out.
* Give each other hickies.
* Hide a jelly bean in your pajamas and dare her to find it.

Remember, it's not just a physical issue. There's a lot of mental and emotional elements as well. Take your time. You also might find that you're not as eager to trot as you once were. Don't sweat it. Birth and a new baby are a big deal. Don't pressure each other. Relax and wait it out.

I REMEMBER SEX . . . THAT THING WE USED TO DO.

It turns out that hormonal changes, breastfeeding, and overall exhaustion can have an impact on some women's libido. This can last a looong time.

Sex after pregnancy can be a real hurdle for a couple. It's like eating. You never stop to think how good it is that you and your partner get hungry at about the same time every day. You never think, "Wow. We are both totally up for eating at least twice a day. Sometimes three times!"

But all of a sudden she's more like, "You know, I'm just not that hungry. Not at all. I could go days, weeks, without eating."

You're starving, and things can get tense.

This can throw a couple for a loop, so be prepared.

• Remember to be affectionate even if you're not trying to get a little sheet-time romance.

• Hold her hand, kiss her in the hall, rub her back—even if you know it won't lead to actual sex. Crazy, we know. But a little snuggling can be great for both of you.

• Try courting your partner. Buy her some flowers, make her a special meal, send her little notes, even ask her out on a date. Think of it as tantric foreplay.

• Be patient with her: Take your time. Pretend you're seventeen and dating a Catholic.

• Perhaps most important of all, talk about it. Tell her what you're feeling. Find out what she's feeling. Just because she's not in the mood doesn't mean she doesn't love you anymore. (Or maybe it does, which is sad, for you. . . . Sorry!)

If the situation really starts to rub on you (or if you're the only one doing any rubbing), consider talking to a counselor or a doctor. Maybe they'll have sex with you.

Just kidding.

HOW TO HAVE SEX WITH YOUR WIFE WHEN SHE DOESN'T WANT TO HAVE SEX

Not into courting or patience? No problem. Here are some steps to guarantee a good time. Or at least an okay time.

#1 Beg.
Try lines like, "Come on, please. I mean, I'm hurting. Pretty please? Look, it's scared stiff. It cries real tears."
You won't be proud, and she won't "respect" you. But come on, what has respect ever gotten you?

#2 Guilt her into sex.
Tell her, "I only want to touch you because of my deep, unending love for you. But if you don't feel that way about me . . . no really, I'm fine. You just worry about yourself. I don't even like sex."

#3 Try sneaking in some sex while she's sleeping.
But beware. Getting caught is super embarrassing.

#4 Pay her for sex.
For some reason cash gets a bad reaction, so try favors or chores. For example: "Honey, I mowed the lawn. Can I get that blowjob now?"
It's a fair deal. You do the dishes. She does you. And it keeps the economy of the household going.

#5 Invest in porn.
With the appropriate porn collection, you won't need her anymore. See how she likes that! Porn is like fast food. It tastes good. It's inexpensive. Easy to get. Hot and greasy. Steaming up the windows while you drive from the store and sometimes you just can't

make it home, so you rip open the bag right there at the traffic light and dive in and people start honking but you don't care even though your car has rolled onto the lawn of a nursing home on Outside Art Day and there's a 92-year-old woman banging on your hood with a watercolor portrait of a squirrel, and you don't even notice 'cause you're wrapped up in your sinful delights and it's sooo good and bad and good and so good-bad and it comes with those little packets of ketchup and tiny salts . . . Whew.

AND NOW BACK TO THE BABY!

In this chapter we talked about soaking an injured perineum, handling depression, sex (or lack thereof), and other challenges of this new fathering gig. And we haven't even gotten to the baby yet.

So let's move on and see about some of the challenges and thrills of having a newborn in your life.

CHAPTER 9

THE FOURTH TRIMESTER

COLIC, SLEEP DEPRIVATION, BREASTFEEDING,
AND WILD VEGAS-STYLE PARTYING

The baby is born and safe at home. Finally things can get back to normal.

Yeah, right.

The fourth trimester is made up of those first months out of the womb when the baby is still basically a slighter larger fetus, and your partner is recovering from nine months of human building, followed by squeezing several pounds of flesh from her naughties. Those first few weeks and months are packed with new challenges and new discoveries for you, your partner, and that new little life you've invited to share your home.

A newborn baby is a miracle, without a doubt. But don't be surprised when this miracle spends its days eating, sleeping, pooping, and crying. A little like college but with less beer.

Let's start with the eating.

144

BREASTFEEDING

We at DadLabs love breast milk. It's incredible for the baby's growing body, helps the developing immune system, and it's not bad in your morning coffee.

Seriously, breast milk is incredible stuff. Although chemists continue to improve upon formula, they have yet to match the complex mixture of fats, proteins, and carbohydrates found in breast milk. And it's much more than just food. Breast milk is packed with all kinds of antibodies, hormones, and active enzymes. In all, there are more than 100 ingredients in breast milk that a baby can't get from formula.

Breast milk is also free! The canned stuff is about $20 for a month's supply, or about $1500 a year.

Add all that to the powerful emotional bonding between Mom and baby, and breast milk beats formula by a mile. Of course in some cases breastfeeding is not possible or isn't the right choice for a couple, and thankfully in those cases formula can be a healthy substitute. But if you can, opt for breastfeeding.

Your job as a dad in those first weeks is to support the breastfeeding as best you can. This might include

- pillow fetching to help with positioning
- cheerleading during those first few tries
- contacting a lactation consultant if needed
- washing pump parts and bottles as needed

Breastfeeding couldn't be more natural, but it's a whole new dance for both the baby and the mom, so it's no surprise that there'll be a few missed steps and the occasional squished toe. Don't worry, they'll get the hang of it.

Once a couple of weeks have passed, and the baby's got the latching thing down, Dad might want to try feeding baby a bottle of pumped breast milk, so he can help with the feeding, especially those that take place in the bleary wee hours. If you wait more than six weeks to introduce baby to bottle, many babies will refuse to take a bottle ever again. Now you might be thinking, "Hell, yeah! Let Mom handle that department." But giving your new child one of those early meals might be too wonderful to pass up. And a little later down the road, when Mom is out having martinis with her girlfriends, being able to give the baby a bottle of breast milk is going to make life a hell of a lot easier for you.

Now when a baby puts milk in one end, something entirely different comes out the other end. Which brings us to . . .

145

POOP:
YOUR NEW FAVORITE TOPIC

Let's talk about poop. You should get used to it. Before having a child, you and your partner might have had lyrical conversations about poetry and politics, but for the next few weeks all that talk will be spent on poop. You'll be excited, thrilled, and confused by the myriad textures, colors, and smells coming out of your baby. Trust us, you'll have moments like this:

- "Honey, come in here and check out this poop!"
- "Oh, that's beautiful. Look at the colors! Did you see the one this morning?"
- "You bet. I posted the photo on my blog."

Don't freak out. You're not developing a fecal obsession (most likely). You and your partner are just fascinated with your new baby, and in those early months, pooping and crying are key ways babies tell us what's going on with their bodies.

WIKIPOOPIA

At DadLabs we've begun the monumental task of documenting all the different displays an open diaper might present. We've called on parents from around the world to share with us what they've seen in the poop bag and how we could best re-create the damage without resorting to actual poop. Here are just a few examples from our ever-growing list.

The Redenbacher: Take some Worcestershire sauce, add a larger scoop of peanut butter (creamy or crunchy), sprinkle in chocolate chips and, of course, corn.

The California Roll: Squeeze out some cookie dough, add a few spoonfuls of guacamole, and top it off with molasses.

Cousin Itt: A handful of frozen spinach. That's it. And it's plenty.

Chocolate Rain: Take some chocolate cocoa cereal and soak it overnight in sour milk. Nice.

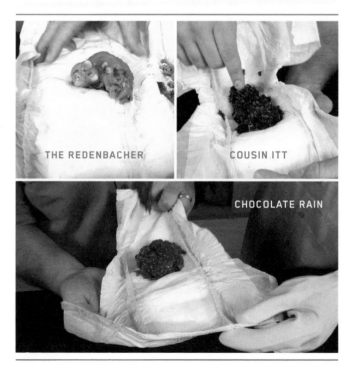

THE REDENBACHER

COUSIN ITT

CHOCOLATE RAIN

THESE ARE THE POOPS OF OUR LIVES

So let's get down to specific kinds of poop.

1.   The first couple of diapers can be scary. The poop is a black, tarry, sticky mess that will leave you feeling like you've just removed a diaper from the *Exxon Valdez*. As we've learned, the stuff is called meconium, and it's perfectly natural (see page 121). It's the tiny bit of waste that's built up in the baby's system while still in the uterus. As the system gets cranked up, the gunk gets pushed out. Kind of like a hot tub.

2.   Next comes the more traditional baby poop. It's mustardy, custardy, and a bit seedy. It barely smells at all or, in some cases, smells like buttered popcorn. Weird, but true. In poop terms, it's actually kind of cute.

3.   Once the baby starts eating solid food (usually somewhere around six months), the poop gets a whole lot nastier. Thicker, smellier, and full of surprises.

DADDYING IS A DIRTY JOB

To paraphrase Spiderman's uncle: With great poop comes great responsibility. Now Dads, changing diapers might not be the most glamorous job in the world of parenting, but for most of us it's an essential chore in baby-raising. Don't you dare try and sneak out of it. Come on, be a man and get your hands and nasal cavities a little dirty.

HOW THE HELL DO I PUT ONE OF
THESE THINGS ON? (PART 2)

You may not believe this, but before long you'll be a diapering wizard, an all-star ass-wiper, a genuine one-man excrement-cleaning service. But to get you started, here are the basic steps on diaper changing once your little bundle is at home. (The earlier hospital version of these instructions was really just a warm-up.)

1.   Gather your supplies. Have a bag or station with your diapers, wipes (alcohol-free for those early weeks), ointments, etc. You don't want a wriggling ball of baby balancing on the changing table and only then discover you left everything in the next room. (Warning: Never leave the baby alone on any high surface. All too often, they find a way down. In fact, never take your eyes, or even one hand, off the little one when he's on the changing table. Babies are squirmy and don't yet know from danger.)

2.   Lay the baby on his or her back. Unclasp the diaper, gently lift up your baby's legs and bottom by pulling up the ankles, and politely comment on the fine digestive work your child has accomplished. Then duck as a yellow arc of baby piss is aimed at your head. This fountain effect is especially frequent for boys. A little exposure to the open air is some kind of signal to the penis that it's time to pee on Dad. Consider it a kind of baptism into fathering.

3.   Once you've got the bottom lifted, clean the offending region. You can use the clean upper part of the diaper to start with, then maybe some baby wipes or some washcloths wet with a little warm water. Remember to wipe front to back. This is especially important for little girls.

4. After cleaning up (don't forget to check under those cute baby fat rolls), you might want to add some baby-rash ointment or baby powder. Occasional use of ointments can really help a baby's nether regions and soothe a diaper rash. There's no need to use ointment every time, unless your doctor has given specific instructions. If you are using baby powder, do not use talcum powder. Talc is bad news for a baby (the particles can be inhaled and may cause respiratory issues).

5. Now for the new diaper. Again, raise the bum-bum by lifting the ankles, slide in the new diaper, and lower the little guy back down. Bring the front panel up and over that adorable belly, and strap it on, firm enough to avoid leaks, but not so tight that the legs turn blue and fall off in the crib.

Of course, you'll soon develop your own stylish technique, but those are the basics. You're going to be told that to successfully change a baby's diaper you'll need four dozen state-of-the-art products and a small, well-funded laboratory. And there are some cool products out there, but in truth, you can get away with a diaper and some wet paper towels. So roll with it. Like we said, you're on your way to being a master of fecal removal. Put that on your resume.

HONEY, I CAN STILL SMELL IT!

No matter your personal choice in diapers or changing technique, you'll most likely need a place to store the dirties. Make sure a quality diaper pail is high up on the baby-shower gift list. We recommend a diaper pail with some kind of sphincter thingy that closes the bag and doesn't let the stank out. This is not the job for your kitchen trash can. We like the Graco Touch-Free Diaper Pail and the Diaper Champ by Baby Trend.

CRYING, SLEEPING, AND SOOTHING

Sleep? Oh yeah, I remember that.

You don't hear much sound from the baby during the first three trimesters, but your kid will more than make up for it in the fourth trimester. A baby will cry for all kinds of reasons: too cold, too hot, too hungry, too gassy, too sleepy, and maybe just for the fun of it. And it can be hard, really hard, on parents. Newborns sleep a lot of hours (14 to 18 hours each day). But they don't sleep these hours all in a row. So prepare yourself. For a while sleep will become as rare and precious as a decent-tasting lite beer. A full night's sleep will become one of those tantalizing legends, like Bigfoot, the Loch Ness Monster, or nude Jamie Lee Curtis pictures.

THE BABY'S AWAKE . . . AGAIN?

As any new parent can tell you, it's absolutely no fun to "sleep like a baby." If long, uninterrupted hours of Zs are your idea of good sleeping, you'll soon discover that newborns are horrible sleepers.

- Our little ones not only take longer to get to sleep, but also have a much shorter sleep cycle (the swing between deep and light sleep), giving them almost twice the amount of lighter, active REM sleep.
- Add this to a tiny belly that wants constant filling, and you've got a squirming, screaming, organic alarm clock living in your house.

This sucks for you, but it works for the baby. Not only does the baby get in some good night feedings, but many researchers believe that the active sleep is healthy for the baby's growing brain. During REM sleep, more blood heads to the brain, and certain vital nerve proteins are formed. Basically, while the body sleeps, the brain is still at the gym building up those mind muscles. This smart sleep is all a part of the massive growth baby experiences in the fourth trimester. So when you're stumbling through your room at 3 A.M., stubbing your toe on the bedpost and spewing a slew of creative four-letter words, just remember: It's for the baby's brain.

IT WON'T STOP CRYING

Holy crap! That screaming, crying sound! It grabs hold of the top of your spin and squeezes. Dads want to run! You'll think, "This baby-having was all my wife's idea. I had nothing to do with it. Come to think of it, the kid doesn't even look like me!" You might want to make a dash for the nearest bar/hardware store/plasma bank/anyplace-but-here. But don't do it. We're parenting here. So stick it out and help soothe.

Yeah, you're going to lose some sleep. Get over it. There's also some hidden treasure in the torture. Rocking your baby back to sleep in the dark, predawn hours can be pure magic. So avoid the temptation to simply hand off to Mom. If she has to deal with every meltdown, you're going to have one burned-out mom on your hands. Share the frustration, share the joy. Be a part of it. Adding Dad to the mix allows the baby to get accustomed to a variety of soothing techniques.

There's no one foolproof way to soothe a baby. Plenty of books and programs offer suggestions that are worth considering, but we advise against subscribing too religiously to any one system. Experiment and find what works for you and your baby. Use several different soothing techniques. This helps the baby be more flexible and teaches her that there's more than one way to calm down.

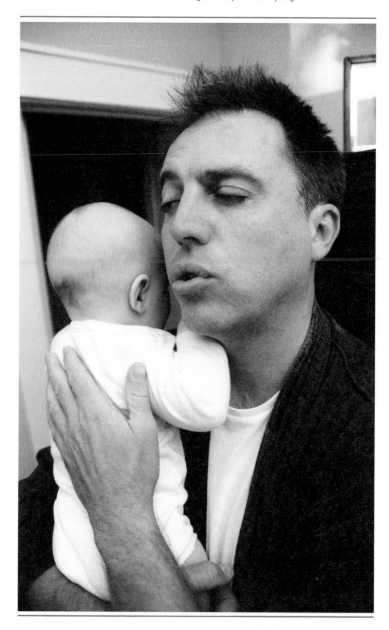

And don't freak out when what the book says doesn't work. Sometimes babies just fuss. Sometimes they just wail their bloody heads off. Colic, in particular, is a bitch.

Some of the techniques we found successful include

• *Singing, humming, and shhing:* It doesn't matter if you've got the voice of Billy Bob Thornton in *Sling Blade,* your baby loves your voice. For extra effect, tuck the baby's head under your chin and let the rumbles of your throat soothe her. And don't worry too much about what you sing: Belt out an old Chicago ballad or something by Michael Bolton. Your baby won't judge your poor taste in music for years to come. If you don't want to sing, a loud shhing can also do wonders. Some doctors think it replicates the white noise from the womb.

• *Squats:* A nice rhythmic set of squats with baby in arms can chill out a screamer. Plus it's a solid thigh workout.

154

• *Swaddling:* Yeah, wrap that baby burrito up. Babies love the tight embrace. Check out the step-by-step box for some tips. We've got some videos on DadLabs.com showing you the swaddling step by steps. You can also Google "swaddling" and find plenty of styles and guides.

• *Walking:* Sometimes a change of environment can do wonders. Take the baby for a walk around the block. Combine this with some singing, and you may simultaneously soothe your crying baby and thoroughly entertain your neighbors.

• *Using the machines:* Many babies find the hum of a car engine or a nearby clothes dryer to be the sweetest sensation this side of the womb. There are also a whole slew of cool swings on the market that offer the hum and the movement to calm the kid.

• *Chilling yourself out:* Your baby picks up on your state of mind. Try going Zen and see if the tyke follows suit.

FIG. A

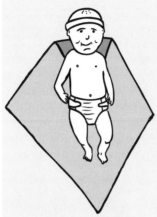

Position baby on blanket as shown, with top corner folded down 4–5 inches.

FIG.B

Wrap right corner under baby's right arm.

FIG. C

Fold up bottom flap to meet the right-arm fold.

FIG.D

Wrap the left corner around baby's body and tuck it into the first fold.

Try a few of these. Some will work, and some will totally fail. Trial and error is the best way to find out. And remember, don't become too dependent on just one method. You want to keep your options open for the day when Michael Bolton songs no longer soothe the raging the child.

LET THE BABY CRY IT OUT?

Experts go back and forth on the self-soothing systems. Here again, we recommend exploring the ideas and deciding for yourself. Trust your instincts.

One thing that experts do agree on: It's impossible to spoil a newborn. Don't worry about picking up and holding your new baby too much. Go ahead and love on that kid to your heart's content. The baby has spent the first nine months of life attached to one of you, so lots of snuggles and cuddles in those first months are going to help her transition into the outer world.

THERE'S A BABY IN MY BED!

There's been a lot of talk on the issue of co-sleeping over the last few years. Many parents find having the baby nestled in the bed with them a comfortable, rewarding sleeping arrangement. Though it's the preference for most of the world's population, co-sleeping has had to wrestle with some negative stigma in the West. But more and more experts are now saying that co-sleeping can be a healthy, happy sleeping situation for both you and your baby.

1. Newborns are delicate creatures. So if you choose to co-sleep, be smart. Avoid blankets that might cover the baby, and if you've been celebrating with a few beers, go sleep on the couch.

2. Some parents feel more comfortable with the baby out of the bed. They want their space and privacy, or simply find they can't relax with baby between them. There are some super-fly cribs out there, ranging from the simple and inexpensive to mini-penthouses with cable television and walk-in closets, so you're sure to find the right one for you.

3. If you're looking for the best of both worlds, check out co-sleeper bassinets like the ones made by Arms Reach. These are cribs that attach to the bed. Kind of like that porch you keep promising to build on the side of the house.

Co-sleeping, crib-sleeping, or something in between is all up to personal preference. Here again, feel it out and go with what works best for your family.

PATERNAL LEAVE:
TAKE A LITTLE TIME

There's a good a chance that your company has a system set up for taking some paternal leave. According to the Family Medical Leave Act in the United States, most employers must offer both their male and female employees twelve weeks of unpaid leave after the arrival of a new child. Many companies provide paid leave as well. Things are even better for new parents in Europe and Canada. In Sweden parents get eighteen months of paid leave. No joke. And at least three of those months are designated for the "minority parent." (More often than not, that's us dads.)

You might be tempted to be the tough guy and pass on the leave, but give it some thought. Being a dad is a job, too. Most men are not wild about spending too much time away from work. We want to keep in the game. Want to be out there providing for our family. But we recommend taking at least a week or two to be at home with your baby and partner. Those first weeks are a precious gift. If you can, make an effort to have nothing in your day planner but your newly enlarged family. If taking time off work isn't possible, make sure you carve out some after-work and weekend hours. Give yourself some hours with nothing to do but hold your new baby. You won't regret it.

HARDER THAN THE PEACE CORPS

The fourth trimester is a wild ride. You and your partner will be learning almost as much as the new arrival. Trust us, there will be some highs and some lows, some moments when you want to do an end zone dance of celebration, and other moments when you'll be asking yourself if you saved the baby receipt. It will be amazing, hilarious, heart-expanding, and hard as hell. Most certainly the toughest job you ever loved. Welcome to Dadhood!

CHAPTER 10

DUTCH TREAT OR MODERN MARRIAGE?

THE 50/50 FINE PRINT

If you find 50/50 odds at a casino in Las Vegas, throw your money on the table, because you have an opportunity to actually win. Unfortunately, this scenario will rarely happen, because the odds of just about every bet you make in Vegas are stacked against you. But this book is not about Vegas; it's about guys and pregnancy. Although living with a pregnant woman is sometimes like gambling in Vegas. You never quite know what the next roll is going to bring.

Rest easy, my friend: While you can't change the outcome of the roll of dice in a Vegas craps game, there is a strategy you can pursue that makes life with the pregnant mom a bit less risky.

What, you ask, can have such a positive impact? Busting up some stereotypes. Trying something new. This strategy does not require us to give up those things that define us as men, though it does force us to change the way we perceive many domestic activities. We advocate that you strive to reach a higher plane of existence, to discover your true self by cleaning toilets, changing diapers, and folding laundry.

We are talking about attaining relationship enlightenment by practicing the 50/50 relationship rule.

WHAT IS THE 50/50 RELATIONSHIP RULE?

Women have achieved a greater equality in the workplace, so they come to marriage and parenting with a new set of expectations. And the ideal is that we share everything equally: 50/50. You can think of this as the flip side of the sexual revolution. The bill for the equality that women have found in the workplace comes due once the baby arrives.

Can couples live up to the ideal of complete equality on the domestic front? If you're scared shitless at this point, you are not alone: 90 percent of men fail the 50/50 test. And for good reason.

Think about where we started. The previous generation of fathers (our dads) somehow got the 95/5 deal. Dad's 5 percent included cutting the grass, grilling hamburgers, and drinking scotch. Any activity that took place indoors, required anything sudsy, or involved any bodily function was women's work.

As descendants of the 5 percenters, many guys today think that, as we get married and have kids, if we go 25 percent we are about five times better than the men who came before us. A reasonable rate of return. While this may be true, our desire to be more involved than our fathers is such that we are called to achieve a higher standard. We are called to live by the 50/50 Relationship Rule! We must do 50 percent of the domestic and parenting work that is required to keep our respective households running smoothly. Welcome to the world of co-parenting.

TIME FOR SOME CHOREPLAY

Although you may never attain a true 50/50 relationship, setting that as a goal will pay dividends.

Why should you seek to take this journey? Maybe it would be better to try and win back your own dad's gig. Get over it, dude. Chicks who accept that crap live in compounds run by religious tyrants. And besides, there are huge benefits to being an equal co-parent.

1. First, as a 50/50 co-parent you will ultimately build stronger relationships with your children than fathers of years past. By being present and taking part in many of the activities that have historically been reserved for moms, you are afforded an opportunity to build intimate relationships with your kids.

YOUR FATHER'S GENERATION: 95/5 parenting

YOUR GENERATION: 50/50 parenting

2. The second and equally important reason for striving for a true 50/50 co-parenting relationship: YOU WILL HAVE MORE SEX. No shit. If you pull your weight around the house, you are much more likely to get laid. This technique for gaining sexual favors, known popularly as "choreplay," works.

As all good self-help books advise, the more frequently you participate in an activity, the more likely it is to become a habit. Thus, the truly enlightened male uses his partner's pregnancy as a time to start his journey. Begin with simple activities during the first trimester of pregnancy and evolve as your partner's pregnancy unfolds. By the time your child arrives, these activities will be established in your inner being, and you will be well on your way to attaining relationship nirvana.

Thusly, your journey to enlightenment and more frequent sexual intercourse begins with the following tasks.

STAGE ONE:
PREGNANCY AND BUILDING THE FOUNDATION

FIRST TRIMESTER ZEN ACTIVITY GUIDE:

1. Place your dirty underwear and socks directly into the dirty clothes hamper without the normal four-day resting period on the floor; generally pick up after yourself.

2. Take over some of the grocery shopping so that the pregnant mom may rest. Make sure you stock up on fruits and vegetables and any other items she is craving. Don't be alarmed at the strange combinations of foods she requests; her palate may rival

that of a drunk coed at 4 A.M. in a dorm room with a can of smoked oysters, some peanut butter, three Twinkies, and a hot plate.

3.   Cook a meal or two. Remember that she will be very sensitive to strong odors, so keep the menu fairly basic and mild. Smoked mackerel and stewed cabbage is not a good choice. One of our wives required that all coffee be brewed in the garage because she was repulsed by the smell, so keep the olfactory issues in mind. Most important, do not be offended if she boots up the entire dinner. This is not a comment on your abilities as a chef.

4.   Assume all animal clean-up duty, especially if you have cats. Although cats are very clean animals, a protozoan called *toxoplasma gondii* is frequently found in their feces. This microbe is benign to healthy adults, but it can cause serious birth defects in unborn children. Exposure to dog poop has not been shown to pose any significant health risks to unborn children. However, picking up Fido's steaming growler is unpleasant enough for those of us with strong stomachs, much less a first-trimester mom who pukes at the smell of daisies.

165

5.   Choose an additional job around the house that she normally does (and hates) and make it yours.

After the first trimester is completed, morning sickness will most likely have subsided (unfortunately for some women, morning sickness lasts the entire pregnancy), her appetite and energy will have returned, and the intense physical symptoms of carrying a close to full-term baby will be several months away. These are the salad days and are a great time for you to work on relationship maintenance. Choreplay may begin to pay off at this point. Many women experience a stimulated libido during the second trimester, so adding a few jobs to your to-do list can pay big dividends here.

SECOND TRIMESTER ACTIVITY GUIDE:

1.   Clean the bathroom. If you have not already taken over this job, do it now. Face it, you are most likely responsible for clogging up the drain with hair and dribbling on the toilet, so take ownership of your thatch and clean up after your disgusting self.

2.   Reestablish date night. Take the initiative and plan a recurring night out. This will be a great time for you to enjoy one-on-one time before the baby arrives. Savor this time together for the next few months, because there will be a date dry spell (among other things) after the baby comes. Date night will ultimately be replaced with soccer practice and homework all too soon, so enjoy.

3.   Learn to fold the laundry. Trust me, this will be huge for you and your status as a sports fan in the future.

4.   Learn to give foot massages. Do it with a smile and thank your lucky stars your ankles are not the size of sterno logs.

THIRD TRIMESTER ACTIVITY GUIDE:

1.   You will be required to assemble a nursery and associated items, such as a crib, changing table, etc.

2.   You should take over jobs Mom cannot physically manage and all those that require strenuous bending or heavy lifting.

3.   You will also be assigned numerous nutty nesting jobs. She will ask you to clean things that are absolutely insane. Do not ask why, just do it. One DadLabber cleaned every air-handling vent in his entire house with a toothbrush, among other things. She will also go on a cleaning frenzy like you have never seen. You will be

puzzled by this turn of events and ask yourself, why the hell did I spend the past eight months doing all of these new chores while my partner, only days away from delivering a child, is able to clean with the vengeance of twelve full-time maids? Do not regret your labors, for she is not in her right mind. Nesting cannot be comprehended by the male mind. You are on a quest, my friend, and all of your labors will ultimately be rewarded.

4. Double your foot massages.

The first phase of your journey to enlightenment is coming to an end. If you have been faithful to your mission, you will have partaken in many activities that most men merely read about, and you will be that much closer to enlightenment. Remember, the point is to dote on your wife as much as possible and to go out of your way to make her life easy. You can't carry the baby for her and experience all of the symptoms of a pregnant woman; you can't go through the excruciating pain of delivering a child; but you can pamper her like no other time in her life.

Gold Nugget: If you have the resources, hire a cleaning service to do all of these jobs. The benefits are similar.

STAGE TWO:
LIFE WITH NEW LIFE

Stage two of your journey begins with the birth of your new child and lasts roughly four to six months. For you and the new mom this can be a difficult time. You will be extremely tired and must face the challenges of caring for a newborn while you are completely exhausted. You must also learn to care for each other in this less than optimal state. When you find yourselves arguing at

2 A.M. about the color of your child's latest diaper, you will know that you are in the depths of stage two. Now is the time for you to hunker down, practice patience, and be supportive of the new mom. This crazy time shall soon pass.

Bottom line, be supportive during the early days—this is where you earn your stripes.

FOURTH TRIMESTER ACTIVITY GUIDE:

1. Continue your prebirth cleaning schedule, letting Mom concentrate on the child.

2. Take your rightful place in the diaper-changing rotation. With several thousand diaper changes in front of you, sharing this duty is essential. You certainly do not want to miss the chance to say to your sixteen-year-old, "I wiped your ass a thousand times when you were little, so don't give me any lip. Be in at 11:30."

3. Learn to soothe your little one when she's crying and screaming. Do not immediately hand off the child when she gets fussy. There is no better feeling than to successfully calm a raging infant and have him fall asleep in your arms. The memory will stay with you forever.

4. Take part in the nighttime feeding ritual. You may not be able to breastfeed, but you can get up and bring the baby to Mom on a rotation basis. This is a great argument to use when she yells at you from a postpregnancy hormone–induced state.

5. Do not miss an opportunity to care for your child in the early days. It provides a great way for you to build a special bond with your son or daughter that will last a lifetime. Most new moms bond immediately with their child at birth, and this is true for

some dads. However, some men have a difficult time connecting with their newborns immediately. Do not fret; bonding increases over time. A wonderful way to speed up the process is to take part in many of the nurturing activities just mentioned.

You must also think of these early weeks as the celibate stage of your journey. There is absolutely no funny business allowed for at least six weeks and sometimes longer. This is a perfect time to ponder inner peace or plant a kick-ass garden.

STAGE THREE:
FROM HERE TO EVER AFTER

Ultimately, things will settle down and return to normal. Well, not the normal you were used to before kids—those days are long gone—but normal from here on out.

* Your child is sleeping through the night.
* Your partner is back to the wonderful lovely person you met and fell in love with.
* You are figuring out the routine of being a father.

At this stage you are halfway up the mountain and are now ready for the third and longest phase of your co-parenting journey. This phase will stretch out well over a decade and will culminate with your sweet little baby leaving home to get a job or go to college, which comes with a big fat tuition bill (but that's another chapter).

The third stage of the journey is the point at which you and Mom begin the co-parenting journey as equals. If you have taken your role seriously during stages one and two, you are likely to be doing more on the domestic front than you ever dreamed possible. You may actually be doing more than Mom at this point, and you may be feeling pretty proud of yourself. Beware of this type of thinking. It is frivolous, egotistical, and extremely dangerous. Unless you have created an incredibly complex carbon-based life form from scratch and nurtured this being inside your body until it developed the ability to survive in a hostile world—and then squeezed this watermelon-sized object out of your body through an aperture the size of a lemon—shut up and humbly begin stage three of your journey, hand in hand with your partner.

The list of all the activities that must be accomplished to keep a family unit running is staggering. The fact that all of these activities must take place outside normal working hours is even more remarkable.

The basic tasks:

Shopping • Cooking • Laundry • Dishes • Bath time • Story time • Tuck-in time • Pickups and dropoffs • Parties • Play dates • Practices • Homework • Handiwork • Yard work • Packing lunches • Getting dressed • Car maintenance • Paying bills • Doctor visits • Family events • School meetings • Etc. • Etc. • Etc.

This list is far from exhaustive but gives you a good idea of the volume of tasks we perform as parents.

LIFETIME ACTIVITY GUIDE:

1. Sit down with your partner and actually write down a list of the things that need to be done to keep the family rolling.

2. Divide the duties between the two of you. This will give each of you a better understanding of just how much work the other is

doing. For example, you will receive the proper credit for yard work, and she will get kudos for writing thank-you notes.

3.   Choose the jobs that include spending time with the kids, such as regularly taking part in bath time and story time. These are wonderful opportunities to interact daily with your children, especially if you leave for work before they get up in the morning.

4.   Choose chores that can be done while watching the game. For example, insist that you will fold the laundry; you can easily do this while watching a game. Never volunteer to do the laundry; if need be, screw up several loads of whites by washing them on hot with some bright colors or wash some delicate items with dirty jeans and several oil rags from the garage. You will be banned from touching the washing machine.

5.   Choose chores that your kids can ultimately take over. Trash and recycling, feeding the animals, and unloading the dishwasher all fall into this category; avoid activities like grocery shopping, which require driving.

6.   Make a big deal out of those activities that are considered gross by the female gender, such as picking up animal waste or cleaning out the shed. Say things like, "Oh my God that was the most foul-smelling dog turd I have ever seen." And describe how it would not easily wipe off the end of the shovel. Appear appalled at the size of the cockroach you saw in the shed. Say, "It was bigger than the rat that was gnawing on the rake." You can use these activities to cancel out her writing thank-you notes.

7.   Immediately volunteer for any chores that are conducive to drinking beer.

By following these simple strategies, you may actually get close to attaining relationship nirvana. You will definitely enhance the relationships with your kids, and you will have more sex than you would have if you sat on your ass all day or constantly played golf. And even though you may never become the perfect father or perfect partner, you can rest easy knowing that you are far, far better than the generations that came before you.

DEVELOPMENTAL SIGNPOSTS

AND OTHER WEAPONS OF MASS DESTRUCTION

- "Well, our baby was crawling by that age."
- "Gosh, your baby is fat. Should she be that fat?"
- "I read that if a baby doesn't blink thirty times a minute, then it will grow dragon wings by the age of two."

Prepare yourself. Along with your baby come growth charts, milestone markers, competitive parents, and more unasked-for advice than an episode of *Oprah*. This chapter covers the cool things your baby will be learning, how to help her learn, what to keep an eye out for, and, most important, how not to freak out.

IT STARTS WITH THE CHARTS

It starts immediately after birth:

- They take your newborn delight and start measuring, weighing, and comparing.
- You're given little growth percentile charts that show the average healthy height-to-weight ratio for newborns on up.
- Suddenly your gurgling miracle is reduced to a set of numbers and a dot on a graph.

Some dads really get into this. It's like watching your stock portfolio grow or following baseball stats. (Or for you nerdy dads, it's like charting your orc sword's demon points.) Others remain neutral until their wives start to obsess about "failure to thrive" and other ambiguous labels pediatricians bandy around. Still others get as anxious if not more anxious than their partners.

And so, the mantra of this chapter is "Don't freak out!" From the start, people will be comparing your baby to other babies, and you'll be asking yourself, "Is my kid normal?" Babies come in all kinds of sizes and ratios: long, fat babies; tiny, hairy babies; even the occasional baby with teeth (it happens!). Your baby's early position on the height/weight ratio chart doesn't tell us much about where that baby is going to end up. Fat babies can grow into skinny kids. Small babies become linebackers. And different babies grow at different rates. If your baby rolls over a little early, it doesn't necessarily mean you can clear a space on the shelf for a future Nobel Prize. Likewise, your baby being a little late hitting a developmental milestone is no cause for panic. Relax.

BUT THE EXPERTS SAY . . .

There is a slew of parenting advice out there: parenting books, medical Web sites, mothers-in-law, childless friends, strangers at grocery stores, etc. These advice-givers will shovel out enough crap to fill your new diaper pail to the rim. They'll explain what your child should be doing, what you should be doing, and the unalterable harm your parenting is wreaking upon your child.

Of course, advice and guidance can be a wonderful gift (you're reading this book, aren't you?). But take all this advice with a grain of salt. In fact, take it all with enough salt to kill a rhino.

Advice from experts, neighbors, and online chat rooms should come with a warning: "May Cause Unnecessary Fear and Guilt." Get on the Internet and you'll find some "expert" telling you something is wrong with your child faster than you can find low-budget porn. Beware of inflammatory statements such as

- your child cries too much
- your child cries too little
- your child cries in the wrong musical key

Often these experts will follow their diagnosis with their one fix-it-all solution: Just enter your credit card number here.

But take care, guys. Babies aren't Chevy trucks with identical Hemi engines. Each baby is unique, with different sleep patterns, growth rates, and feeding styles. Individuality started when your sperm did a break-in and entry on the egg. Don't let the fear mongers (even well-meaning fear mongers) convince you that something is dreadfully wrong with your child because she is other than average. Ironically, a completely average child is a rare find— which goes against the averages. Remember, you and your partner are the only true experts. No one knows your baby and your baby's needs better than you.

KIDDIE KOMPETITION

Sure, you could resist the urge to compete with every parent on the planet. But why? If you don't compete, how can you win? Here are some simple ways to win the parenting game.

1. Buy a few stroller bumper stickers that read, "My Child's Height-to-Weight Ratio Is Closer to Average Than Your Child's." Available at most hospital gift stores. Buy a few.

2. Enroll your newborn in online college courses.

3. So maybe your two-week-old isn't walking yet, but with a little creative Photoshopping you can upload a picture of your new-

born sprinting the hundred-yard dash. If you invest in some CGI software, there's no telling what your child can accomplish.

4. When no one's around, tell other people's kids they're stupid.

5. Replace your child's lullaby CD with motivational lectures. Tony Robbins is a good starter.

6. Have guests over and make sure the baby monitor is on full volume. From the nursery play a recording of you reciting T. S. Elliot's poetry in a baby voice. When your guests gasp and ask if your baby is reading poetry, shrug and answer, "Only the modernists."

7. When people compliment your baby's cute knit hat, say, "Thanks. He made it himself."

8. If, while visiting another family's house, you find "World's Cutest Kid" cups, frames, or T-shirts, destroy them.

9. When a fellow father announces he has to change the baby's diaper, look disgusted and ask, "Is he still crapping himself?"

10. Wake your baby every morning to the theme from *Rocky*.

11. When an excited mom or dad announces a new developmental milestone for their child, look bored and reply, "Oh yes, I remember when our little one did that. It was thrilling . . . at the time."

DEVELOPMENTAL MILESTONES

"Honey, look what the baby just did!"

At first it poops, it cries, it sleeps, it wriggles . . . and that's about it. Your child is a blob of flesh that you love with all your heart, but quickly the baby starts learning, developing, and changing. The baby is waving her arms, moving her eyes, nodding her head. To the casual observer she looks like a sorority girl with a wine-cooler hangover, but in truth the baby is working out muscle motor skills, learning to use her new eyes, and beginning to perfect the lifelong skill of holding her head up. It's Human School, and the homework is intense.

MOTOR SKILLS AND EXPLORATION

Belly time is an exhilarating workout for your baby in her first few months: Place her belly-down on a blanket and watch her learn:

1. She'll last for brief periods at first, but longer as she grows.

2. She'll learn to push herself up and support herself with her arms.

3. Her wobbly head will begin to steady out.

4. She'll learn to lift her head and look around.

Back time is great, too. She'll start grasping at dolls and fingers or swiping at toys like a clumsy cat. Watch how she learns to grip and starts squeezing your nose or her own. Let her kick and punch. If you have friends with babies, line them up, put on some techno music, and watch the Baby Rave burn!

HEARING SKILLS: IT'S ALL NEW

Most likely your baby has heard your voice long before birth. If you're reading this before the big day: Talk to that belly! Tell that baby you're looking forward to seeing her face. When she comes out, she'll have a familiar voice to greet her.

Many hospitals offer a hearing screening test in the first hours after birth. If there's a problem, a second test is scheduled. (Often a newborn fails the initial hearing test due to middle ear fluid, or gunk in the ear canal, or simply because they're crying.)

Once you have your baby home, watch how he responds to the common sounds of the world. Footsteps, voices, music, creaky doors—they're all new! And baby is learning to respond.

Many parents find that their baby is calmed by the sounds of a fan, vacuum cleaner, or a recording of ocean surf. Some experts believe this is because the sounds simulate the white, surflike noise of the womb. That might explain why a loud, calm "shhhhh" from a parent helps soothe a crying baby.

VISION: OBJECTS ARE CLOSER THAN THEY APPEAR

A newborn usually has a focus range of about twelve inches, which is perfect for a baby cradled in your arms and looking up at your face. Remember, she's been in the womb her whole life till now. The world has suddenly gotten a lot bigger. It's like moving out of the dorm and into St. Paul's Cathedral. It takes a while to adjust.

Soon your baby will start checking out designs, contrast shades, even colors. It's fun to try to watch what she's watching. You might walk into a coffee shop and see Mel Gibson mugging the Beastie Boys, but to your baby the most exciting thing in the room is the ceiling fan. Babies love ceiling fans!

Another fun moment to notice is the day your child discovers her hands or feet. "What the hell are these things? Wait a second, that's what I've been touching stuff with?"

Sometimes watching your baby is like hanging out with a friend on one long mushroom trip: "Wow. All the colors. Have you ever just watched your hand, man?"

COMMUNICATION: TRIAL RUNS

Baby learns to communicate long before speaking. A baby learns to smile in her first months, then learns to laugh and read facial expressions. Many babies will begin mirroring your expressions, but the smarty-pants daddy-mimicking may take a few months.

- Try facing your baby and sticking out your tongue.
- Watch as she learns to do the same thing.
- It won't be too long before your baby reaches out for you—her way of saying she needs you.
- Go ahead and mop up your melted heart—and pick her up.

HOW CAN I HELP?

Want to help your newborn learn and grow?

1. Play with her.

2. Spend time holding her.

3.   Let the baby explore your face with her hands and eyes. Believe it or not, you and your partner's faces are two of her favorite sights in the world. This won't be the case when she turns sixteen, so enjoy it while it lasts.

4.   Talk to your child. Tell her about the world around her. She'll dig it. She might even respond with coos. Have a conversation of sounds. Tell her about textures and smells. She might have a vocabulary of zero, but she's learning tones and emotions.

5.   Sing to her. Don't worry if you haven't got a great voice. It never stopped Ringo.

6.   Offer her toys to grasp or your fingers to squeeze. Follow her interests.

7.   Hold her facing out from your body, letting her see the world. Then follow her eyes and walk in that direction. She'll lead to unexpected treasures in a room you thought you knew.

8.   Cradle and comfort that crying child. She's trying to tell you something. The experts agree: You can't spoil a newborn baby!

There will be huge changes for your baby over the next two years: sitting up on her own, standing, crawling, first solid foods, first steps, first words, and on and on. With each milestone your and your baby's worlds are changed. Enjoy the ride!

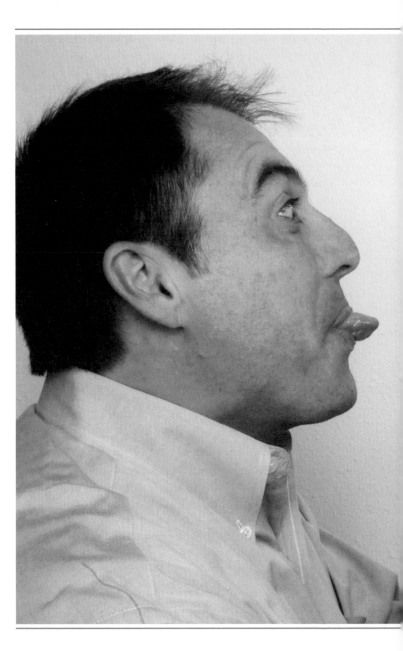

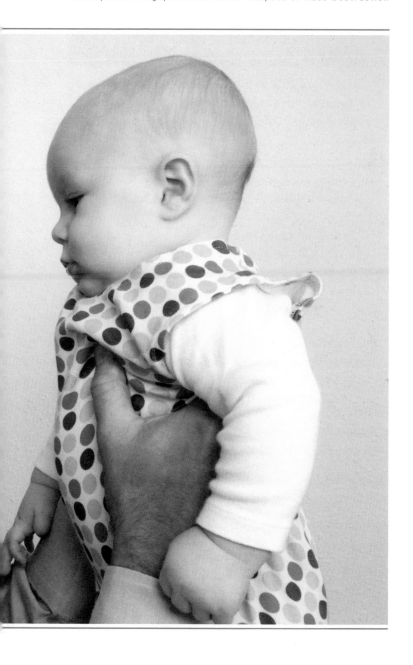

KEEPING AN EYE OUT

Remember what we said? Babies develop at different rates. Your child might be a few steps ahead of the curve, or a few behind. It's all natural. But it is good to keep an eye out for signs that your baby is struggling.

1. If you find your three-month-old is not trying to lift her head or seems over-floppy, you'll want to talk to your pediatrician.

2. Perhaps your baby isn't focusing on your eyes or responding to touch and noise—again, talk to the doctor.

3. The same is true for a child who is having trouble gaining weight in those early months.

Again, no one knows your child better than you and your partner. So listen to your gut. If you think something might need attention, ask your doctor. But even then: Don't freak out.

Many children struggle through developmental milestones. Sometimes it's a case of late-blooming; other times the issue is more serious. Early detection of hearing, visual, or motor skill impairment can help a child receive the necessary care.

184

LEARNING TO LEARN FROM THE LEARNER

Remember that friend who one night confessed to never having seen *Star Wars*? Remember how you dashed over to the video store and forced him to watch it that very night? Remember how cool it was to be there when someone was experiencing the *Star Wars* galaxy for the first time?

Just think how much more that's true for your newborn. She is in awe of wind. She's feeling cotton for the first time. The smell of cut grass is completely new. Watch her, learn from her. She is experiencing a fresh wonder that we have forgotten.

INDEX

ACKNOWLEDGMENTS

The guys in the lab coats would like to thank:

Bill Crawford for his help in the distillation process. Mindy Brown, Mary Ellen Wilson, and the great folks at Quirk for lighting the pilot. Tim and Phyllis Hall, Courtney Nichols, Bud and Barbara Nichols, Carol and John Garey, Hillis Lanier, Marcus Soper, Richard Whitley, Bill Rogers, and Daylight Partners for keeping the beakers bubbling. Thanks to our parents for passing on their own results (in so many ways).

Most of all we want to thank our intrepid Lab Partners—Jodi, Kim, Liz, and Miriam—for standing with us throughout these experiments. And thanks to the Lab Rats—Wilson, Riley, Cooper, Walker, Ella, Carson, Maya, Arden, and Oscar—for being such good test subjects. We love you guys.